THE
COLORS
OF
LOVE

THE
COLORS
OF
LOVE

GETTING TO KNOW
YOUR ROMANTIC SELF
THROUGH COLOR

DR. MAX LÜSCHER

Translated by
Jennifer Francesca Dozio

St. Martin's Press ✹ New York

First published in Germany. Copyright © 1995 F. A. Herbig Verlagsbuchhandlung GmbH, München. © 1995 Color-Test-Verlag AG, Luzern.

Design by Nancy Resnick

Library of Congress Cataloging-in-Publication Data

Lüscher, Max.
    [Farben der liebe. English]
    The colors of love : getting to know your romantic self
through color / by Max Lüscher; translated by Jennifer F. Dozio.
        p.   cm.
    ISBN 0-312-14295-1
    1. Love.   2. Color—Psychological aspects.   I. Title
BF575.L8L8713   1996
306.7—dc20   96-511
                                                         CIP

First U.S. Edition: June 1996

10 9 8 7 6 5 4 3 2 1

CONTENTS

THE
COLORS
OF
LOVE

1

■ ■ ■ ■ ■ ■ ■ ■ ■

HOW COLOR CAN DETERMINE YOUR ROMANTIC TYPE

■ ■ ■ ■ ■ ■ ■ ■ ■

Have you ever noticed that the feeling you get when you look at a square object is somehow different from the feeling you get when you look at a circle? Architects, for example, are very much aware of the role that shapes play in our lives. A tall, rectangular building with sharp right angles will appeal to you, on some level, in a completely different way from a building constructed with only smooth, round edges.

You might not know it, but the same phenomenon that holds true for shapes is also true for colors. As any artist can tell you, the feeling you get from a certain shade of red is not the same feeling you experience when you look at a deep blue. You experience every new color differently and in your own individual way.

In much the way sound waves can be measured on different frequencies, colors can produce a visible and precisely measurable, sensual experience. From these measurements an objective chart of your own personal color-sensory experience can be established to reflect qualities about your romantic self.

The color test presented in this book is a sensitive instrument, like a thermometer. Through this test, your personal reaction to a color reveals your subjective feelings, much the same way a thermometer records temperature. Thus, the color test is an *objective* way of measuring your *subjective* mental and physical state.

This test is specifically designed to free you of your verbal inhibitions and to discover your subconscious color preferences, which can help determine your romantic profile. It is *not* just another questionnaire where you can manipulate the answers to show yourself as you want to be seen.

> Research at American and European Universities (including blood, cardiovascular, endocrinological, neurophysiological tests, and electrocardiograms) has shown that with the Clinical Lüscher Color Test an exact psychological, medically verifiable, profile of the total person can be drawn.

EVALUATING YOUR COLORS OF LOVE

Directions:

1. Cut out the four color cards following page 54 and position them against a light background.

2. Ask yourself: How do I experience my erotic/love relationships? Then ask yourself: Which one of these colors:

   Best matches my experience?
   Place the color card at the top of your background.
   Second best?
   Place this color card below the first.

*The least?**
   Place this color card below the second.

3. Turn your cards over and read the numbers from top to bottom. Match your results with the sets on the following pages.

   The last number has been printed smaller so you can find your chart more easily.

Caution:
   The question must always be "Which of these colors best represents my erotic/love relationship?" If you're asking yourself "Which of these colors do I like best?" then you're cheating yourself out of an accurate reading!

---

*Note: This should *not* be your third choice. This card should be the one color of the four which least expresses your erotic/love relationships.

2

THE COLORS OF
YOUR ROMANTIC
EXPERIENCE

In the last seven years researchers have discovered four specific colors that can be used to measure your erotic/love experience and to discover your romantic self. We'll call them the Colors of Love.

Each of these colors represents a particular element of your sexuality:

> Number 1—Deep Purple: devotion and
>   bonding
> Number 2—Magenta: resonance
> Number 3—Orange: sexual arousal
> Number 4—Cinnamon pink: fantasies and
>   expectations

Once the field was narrowed to these four colors, a test group of 3,740 people was asked the following questions:

How do you experience your erotic/love
relationships?
Which one of these colors best matches your
experience? Second best? The least?

If you think the answers would be the same across the
board, you're in for a big surprise! One person might look
at the color orange and find his feelings matched exactly—
he sees the fire and passion of the erotic relationship. The
same person looks at the deep purple and feels nothing
at all. Seated next to him might be a woman who, when
she thinks of love, relates to the color purple. The fiery
orange just turns her off. It makes her think of soulless
sex, not the deeply emotional erotic love she relates to. As
ong as you keep your erotic/love relationships in mind,
your color choice will always remain the same.

The Colors of Orgasm

The physical effects of orgasm have already been
measured, filmed, and shown on television. The
stages of excitement have been plotted into a definite curve. On the other hand, the emotional experience of an orgasm is best described through
color.

Roughly a quarter of us dreams in color. A
few people have also been know to experience

---

color hallucinations during orgasm. For the past few decades, statistically proven studies by the Austrian psychiatrist Herwig Sausgruber have shown that interpretation of a dream is, without exception, dependent on the color experienced or associated with that dream. So, for example, highly arousing or aggressive situations are always dreamed in red.

If color sensations are experienced during the course of an orgasm, they usually occur at the high point of increasing excitement and stimulation.

Color experiences during orgasm begin with the color magenta, which we have numbered as erotic color #2. The psychological meaning of magenta is expressed as the sensitive state of excitement at which strong attractions are established. Therefore magenta means that you are ready to create a resonance with your partner as well as erotic fascination and spiritual connection.

As your excitement grows and escalates into physical sensations, magenta becomes a true red.

On the next level of excitement red changes into a yellowed shade of orange-red. We've numbered this erotic color #3. This longer-lasting phase of excitement is considered a plateau. The next phase is much shorter and involves incredible tension and contraction of the muscles. The measurement of this contraction occurs as a deep blue-green. The peaking tension falls quickly into resolution. This phase is also short, and is represented by a pale yellow. (The blue-green color of the contraction phase and the pale yellow of the resolution phase are *near* the orange and deep purple of the four basic colors in the Clinical Lüscher Color Test.)

The resolution phase (yellow) is followed by a longer-lasting phase of peaceful relaxation. This phase is expressed by deep purple, which we have numbered erotic color #1.

THE ROMANTIC TYPE CHARTS

From the four Colors of Love and their various meanings we can describe twenty-four different romantic types. Once you know which colors you really connect with, as well as your order of preference, you can discover your true romantic type by reading from a simple chart.

However, don't be fooled by how simple this seems. The color choices and romantic Type Charts reveal a lot more than just sexual feelings. They describe your complete emotional experience. If you and your partner discover that your color choices are the same you'll realize that you're truly "on the same wavelength"!

A couple I knew had decided to get a divorce. During our counseling sessions I had tried and tried, without success, to uncover their hidden conflicts, or other understandable reasons for their decision. Finally I asked them to take the Color Test, and once I examined the results it all became clear. Their Romantic Type Charts revealed that they experienced their relationship in completely different ways.

The Romantic Type Chart doesn't describe which sexual practices you prefer or whether you are heterosexual or homosexual; instead it gives you a picture of what emotions you experience and how you perceive your sexual relationships.

The language of colors is a language of the senses, of feelings and perceptions. In music every half-note has a tangibly different effect. Colors are much the same. Every shade offers a different, but definite, range of sensations. Just as music expresses a variety of emotional states, the language of colors paints an immeasurably rich yet precise picture of experiences and feelings.

Anyone who understands the importance of emotional experience and realizes how pressing a mentally and physically fixed outlook can be knows that spoken language is somehow not designed to express such deep feelings. This is perhaps the main reason why in this field verbal counseling or psychotherapy can sometimes do little or nothing at all to help the patient. Sometimes color can speak louder and more clearly than words.

Romantic Type Chart   ■ 1
                                           ■ 2
                                           ■ 3

You are not a sexual go-getter. You're a sensitive partner with a distinct need for peace and harmony. Your way of experiencing an erotic/love relationship is through a deeply felt sympathy. An emotional bond and trusting connection with your partner are prerequisites to an erotic/love relationship. Your particular gifts are your delicately receptive, resonant way of connecting with your partner and your readiness for tender devotion.

Sexual Excitability	■				
Fantasy Expectations	■	■			
Resonance	■	■	■		
Bonding Ability	■	■	■	■	

Romantic Type Chart

■ 1
■ 2
■ 4

An honest and open partnership is worth a lot to you. You have a distinct need for peace and harmony. Your definition of a love/ erotic relationship is a binding sense of "belonging together," which makes you ready and willing to "go for it" with complete abandon. Your feelings are loving, tender, and sensitive. In your partnerships you work toward a harmonious, mutual under- standing and a faithful bond. A relationship built for the long term is important to you, through which you can create a delicate resonance with your partner.

Superficial relationships, pursued only to boost your self- image and lived as short-term sexual adventures, are empty and meaningless for you.

Sexual Excitability	■	■			
Fantasy Expectations	■				
Resonance	■	■	■		
Bonding Ability	■	■	■	■	

Romantic Type Chart

■ 1
■ 3
■ 2

Somewhere in your past is a relationship gone bad—and let's face it, it really shook you up! This nasty experience has really influenced the way you approach eroticism and love. Disillusionment has taken the place of romantic expectations. In order not to make the same mistake twice, you've become very critical and careful. You're avoiding emotional attachment like the plague but you still place a great deal of importance on peaceful harmony in a relationship. What you're looking for is a guarantee of a trusting bond in your relationship. Once your criteria are met, you are more than ready to embark on a lustful, exciting, and sensually warm experience.

Sexual Excitability	■	■	■		
Fantasy Expectations	■	■			
Resonance	■				
Bonding Ability	■	■	■	■	

Romantic Type Chart

■ 1
■ 3
■ 4

There are a lot of different ways of experiencing love and erotic relationships. Your general experience is one of bonding, faithfulness, and exclusivity to your partner. Your greatest need is for peaceful harmony and mutual trust, which are absolute prerequisites for you. Your need for "oneness" is less a product of rules you've set for yourself than an actual part of your personality and of how you fall in love.

So when your prerequisites for a loving bond and faithful feeling of "belonging together" have been fulfilled, you can experience and delight in real sensual warmth and lustful excitement.

Sexual Excitability	■	■			
Fantasy Expectations	■				
Resonance	■	■			
Bonding Ability	■	■	■	■	■

Romantic Type Chart   ■ 1
                         ■ 4
                         ■ 2

A deep disappointment in a past experience has strongly affected the way you approach erotic relationships. Because of this you don't really believe that perfect understanding is possible between two partners and you can't imagine that two people ever really connect on exactly the same wavelength. However, you're also not the kind of person who enters a relationship only to find intensive sexual excitement. Your definition of love is a conflict-free relationship, lived in peaceful harmony with your partner. You're not the type to stage jealous rages and breakups, and they won't be a part of your relationship if you can help it. What you need is a partnership in which you can find mutual trust and love.

Sexual Excitability	■	■			
Fantasy Expectations	■	■	■		
Resonance	■				
Bonding Ability	■	■	■	■	

Romantic Type Chart

■ 1
■ 4
■ 3

Because of your weak self-esteem, the spontaneous, vital quality of your erotic relationships is somewhat hampered. This prevents you from experiencing spontaneous, lusty, sexual excitement or exquisitely impulsive passion.

Your definition of love includes peaceful, caring, and attentive "oneness" with your partner. Your deepest wish in a loving relationship is for harmonious and lighthearted happiness. Living with a partner who can offer this kind of security will help to ease the fears and restraints you've developed for yourself by providing you with a stable, reassuring, and conflict-free environment.

Sexual Excitability	■				
Fantasy Expectations	■	■	■		
Resonance	■	■			
Bonding Ability	■	■	■	■	

Romantic Type Chart   ▨ 2
                       ▨ 1
                       ▨ 3

You're a careful person by nature. This, paired with your high level of erotic sensitivity, tends to hold you back from being spontaneous and taking the direct approach. Especially when you're with someone new, you tend to wait for your partner's erotic signals before making a move of your own. The way you experience your erotic/love relationships is through a delicate receptiveness to your partner's needs and desires. You have a real sixth sense for gauging your partner's excitement, and for knowing how to guide and fire the passion. This talent makes you a truly desirable lover.

You are never one to exert pressure in a relationship. Instead, you believe that both partners must be ready to give. Goal-oriented selfishness (sexual or otherwise) is completely unsexy in your eyes, and always leads to a lack of fulfillment.

Sexual Excitability	■				
Fantasy Expectations	■	■			
Resonance	■	■	■	■	■
Bonding Ability	■	■	■		

Romantic Type Chart

■ 2
■ 1
■ 4

Through your talent for sensitivity and tenderness you're able to truly focus on your partner. This gives your erotic/love relationships a deep and emotional meaning. You're especially good at gauging the excitement of your partner, and knowing how to stimulate and tantalize even more. Your tenderness is fascinating and makes you into a desirable lover. A person who is ready for an erotic bond will find an incredibly satisfying and fulfilling relationship with you and your ability to foster loving devotion allows you to build lasting partnerships.

Sexual Excitability	■	■			
Fantasy Expectations	■				
Resonance	■	■	■	■	
Bonding Ability	■	■	■		

Romantic Type Chart

■ 2
■ 3
■ 1

Your knack for creating an aura of intoxicating, erotic fascination is one in a million. Your desires are intense and so is your way of experiencing the thrill of temptation. These intense appetites are whetted by your ability to be easily aroused. But your predatory, vibrant eroticism never leads you into meaningless sex. Instead, you experience each new relationship as an exciting seduction full of magic and fascination.

Sexual Excitability	■	■	■		
Fantasy Expectations	■	■			
Resonance	■	■	■	■	
Bonding Ability	■				

Romantic Type Chart   ■ 2
                                         ■ 3
                                         ■ 4

Your desire for excitement and to experience the thrill of temptation is easily fired up. However, your intense eroticism rarely leads you to meaningless sex. Instead, desire is a new experience each time for you and it continues to be a magical, growing intoxication every new time you experience it. You are in tune with your own physical and sensual needs and you're always attentive to your partner's excitement. This ability to concentrate on needs and desires allows you not only to continuously reach the highest levels of excitement and arousal but also enables you to create a close, satisfying, and mutually engaging bond with a partner who can match your intensity.

Sexual Excitability	■	■	■		
Fantasy Expectations	■				
Resonance	■	■	■	■	
Bonding Ability	■	■	■		

Romantic Type Chart   ■ 2
                       ■ 4
                       ■ 1

Your erotic experiences are the unique and exciting result of your rich and lively fantasy life. Desire wakens your playful side and each encounter becomes one of many exciting, interchangeable erotic scenarios. You use your fantasies as fascinating, exciting, and fulfilling expressions of your inner desire. Hard-core kinky sex or technically "perfect" sex means less to you than the charm of original and imaginative lovemaking.

Sexual Excitability	■	■			
Fantasy Expectations	■	■	■		
Resonance	■	■	■	■	
Bonding Ability	■				

Romantic Type Chart

■ 2
■ 4
■ 3

You are definitely not a sexual predator. Instead, you live in your own world of erotic desires and romantic scenarios. While your more vital and spontaneous instincts are held back, you're able to develop incredibly rich, delicate fantasies, and these erotic scenarios are your main way of experiencing excitement and fulfillment. Your caring tenderness and deeply emotional eroticism are especially appealing to sensitive, like-minded lovers.

Sexual Excitability	■				
Fantasy Expectations	■	■	■		
Resonance	■	■	■	■	■
Bonding Ability	■	■			

Romantic Type Chart   ■ 3
                          ■ 1
                          ■ 2

You experience eroticism as a hot, temperamental state of excitement. Yet your ideas of sexuality have been deeply affected by negative past experiences. You're disillusioned and mistrust any kind of romantic, artificial gushing. You protect yourself by being highly critical, reserved, and by not allowing yourself to become emotionally dependent on anyone. What you're really looking for in a relationship is not sexual fulfillment, but a solid, friendly, conflict-free, and mutually supporting partnership.

Sexual Excitability	■	■	■	■	
Fantasy Expectations	■	■			
Resonance	■				
Bonding Ability	■	■	■		

Romantic Type Chart

■ 3
■ 1
■ 4

Your definition of erotic love is not just temperamental sexual fulfillment but also a condition of friendly, understanding, and mutually supportive bonding. You tend to bond very closely with your partners, and this allows you to experience a deeply emotional, sensuous, warm, and tender relationship. Multiple partners and superficial sexual relationships without the benefit of emotional bonding are just not your cup of tea. They're too empty and meaningless.

Sexual Excitability	■	■	■	■	
Fantasy Expectations	■				
Resonance	■	■			
Bonding Ability	■	■	■		

Romantic Type Chart   ■ 3
                              ■ 2
                              ■ 1

Your definition of eroticism is essentially one of temperamental desires, lustful fantasies, and arousing fascinations. At the tiniest erotic signal from a partner or in an exciting situation, you respond with almost instant arousal. Your desire for excitement and for the experience of a sexual "high" is very easily awakened. You have a way of magically creating attraction through your spontaneity. You always seem ready to join the fun! (This makes you very attractive to prospective partners.) The excitement you create makes simple desire grow to intoxicating arousal and lets the most intense sensual experiences unfold.

Sexual Excitability	■	■	■	■	■
Fantasy Expectations	■	■			
Resonance	■	■	■		
Bonding Ability	■				

Romantic Type Chart

■ 3
■ 2
■ 4

Your response to seductive signals from your partner or to suggestive situations is strong erotic excitement. Your temperamental and spontaneous readiness to "join the fun," to experience the intoxication of arousal, comes partly from being in tune with your own physical needs and partly from your ability to sense your partner's needs and excitement. Despite your desire for conquest and seduction, you don't go for superficial, promiscuous sexual relationships. Instead you let your sexual intensity and fantasies unfold in a bonded partnership.

Sexual Excitability	■	■	■	■	
Fantasy Expectations	■				
Resonance	■	■	■		
Bonding Ability	■	■			

Romantic Type Chart ■ 3
                     ■ 4
                     ■ 1

*You experience eroticism as an intoxicating storm of lusty sce-
narios and physical thrills. You are easily excited and your excitement is never held back by critical reservations or shyness.
Your desires are strong, impulsive, and easily fired up. Your
experience of seduction and sexual contact is one of carefree play
and thrilling adventure.*

Sexual Excitability	■	■	■	■	■
Fantasy Expectations	■	■	■		
Resonance	■	■			
Bonding Ability	■				

Romantic Type Chart

■ 4
■ 1
■ 3

You have low self-esteem and you don't believe that you might be erotically appealing. This makes you cautious and insecure, especially when you meet someone who seems to fulfill your aesthetic requirements and high expectations. You tend to idealize this person on the level of romantic fantasy—and you hope they'll take the initiative, though your erotic desires are not for passionate, temperamental sex. You express yourself through visual attentiveness as a sign of your deeply felt emotional attachment and love.

Sexual Excitability	■				
Fantasy Expectations	■	■	■	■	
Resonance	■	■			
Bonding Ability	■	■			

Romantic Type Chart   ▨ 3
                       ▨ 4
                       ▨ 2

Your ideas of sexuality have been scarred by negative experiences in the past. You don't really believe that two people can have a profound, emotional understanding, or that they can truly be on the same wavelength. You're deeply disillusioned and you protect yourself by being constantly on guard against emotional dependence upon another person. However, you experience sex as carefree fun, as a provocative game, or as an adventure with no strings attached. In your sexual relationships you're neither critically reserved nor do you attach any importance to choosiness or restraint.

Sexual Excitability	■	■	■	■	■
Fantasy Expectations	■	■	■		
Resonance	■				
Bonding Ability	■				

Romantic Type Chart
■ 4
■ 1
■ 2

Your approach to sexuality has been deeply affected by negative experiences in the past and by your insecurities in the face of erotic relationships. As a result, you've become disenchanted and critical. You don't really believe that a mutual understanding can be reached with another person, or that two people can really be on the same wavelength. You protect yourself with skeptical reservation and by avoiding any kind of emotional dependence. You tend toward pleasant and aesthetically appealing partners. Your relationships are usually sexually desirable and exciting situations but remain uncompromising and undemanding.

Sexual Excitability	■				
Fantasy Expectations	■	■	■		
Resonance	■				
Bonding Ability	■				

Romantic Type Chart

■ 4
■ 2
■ 1

You are not a sexual go-getter. You'd rather hold back and observe from the sidelines with desiring and insecure eyes. Your erotic wishes are fired up by aesthetically pleasing appearances. You have created your own personal ideals and you develop these images and emotions with romantic fantasies. You believe that to win the affection you so deeply desire, you have to make yourself charming and attractive and to create an atmosphere of mutual attentiveness.

Sexual Excitability	■				
Fantasy Expectations	■	■	■	■	■
Resonance	■	■	■		
Bonding Ability	■				

Romantic Type Chart   ■ 4
                       ■ 2
                       ■ 3

The minute you meet somebody attractive who seems to fulfill your desires, you begin to idealize that person and to develop these images with romantic fantasies. However, because you idealize this person, you're held back and you remain yearningly hesitant. You believe that to win the affection you so deeply desire, you have to make yourself charming and attractive and to create an atmosphere of mutual attentiveness.

Sexual Excitability	■				
Fantasy Expectations	■	■	■	■	
Resonance	■	■	■		
Bonding Ability	■	■			

Romantic Type Chart

■ 4
■ 3
■ 1

Your erotic desires are easily and quickly fired up when you meet someone who is particularly aesthetically pleasing and attractive. This kind of encounter creates a spontaneous desire, despite which you remain hesitant. Because you idealize this person you tend to hold yourself back. However, as soon as a feeling of trust is established, you can thoroughly delight in sensuousness. Through your penchant for romantic fantasy, your erotic relationship is constantly being enriched.

Sexual Excitability	■				
Fantasy Expectations	■	■	■	■	
Resonance	■	■	■		
Bonding Ability	■	■			

Romantic Type Chart

■ 4
■ 3
■ 2

Your unfulfilled expectations of how the ideal and lustful rela-
tionship should play itself out have resulted in a nasty experience
that has scarred your ideas of partnership and sexuality. Because
of this you've become disillusioned, critical, and very careful. You
don't really believe that a deeply emotional mutual understanding
can occur between two people. You protect yourself by being skep-
tical and reserved and by avoiding emotional dependence at all
costs. You tend to be more attracted to and impressed by aes-
thetically pleasing situations and objects.

Sexual Excitability	■	■	■		
Fantasy Expectations	■	■	■	■	
Resonance	■				
Bonding Ability	■	■			

3

UNDERSTANDING THE MANY FACES OF LOVE

The purpose of your life is to experience happiness.

I am not saying that as an optimist peering through rose-colored glasses, rather as a thoughtful realist. I won't be led into error by empty platitudes and opinions that I haven't arrived at through my own observation and that don't reflect my own experience. I believe we should take particular care to protect ourselves from political and religious pressures and dogma. We shouldn't allow ourselves to become dependent on either concepts or social/status symbols.

In this book we—you and I—are trying to understand the many aspects of love. However, we also want to free ourselves from dependencies that only lead us into dead ends.

About twice a year, I hold a seminar for a few days in a hotel in an attractive, scenic setting.

The twenty or so participants are always from different

professions and walks of life, and include physicians, teachers, journalists, and businesspeople. A few are directly involved in the practice of pain management. What I really like about the participants is their humanness, their desire to seek the truth, their humor, and their healthy common sense.

Nobody comes to "preach" to one another, and above all we do not come together to moralize. We simply try to reach meaningful insights through group discussion. Each person brings what he or she can to the discussion. Technically I am the seminar leader, but I am not there to instruct like a schoolteacher. On the contrary, I try to avoid lecturing at all costs. I try to encourage the participants to consider and think carefully about questions or issues they hold dear, so that they might find a solution on their own. I find the discussions quite helpful also on a personal level. They enable me to see through certain conflicts with clarity and to find solutions to my questions. Once I have cleared these things up, then I am able to handle myself correctly and to avoid unnecessary concerns.

I won't take the time here to introduce all of the participants by name. However, I will introduce—by first name—those whose opinions and questions I bring up in the course of the following chapters.

LOVE

As I ran down the list of possible topics for discussion, Sam—our youngest participant—immediately voiced his interests: "Love would be an interesting topic. As a matter of fact, I already have a problem to discuss."

"Sure," I said. "Tell us about your problem."

Without hesitating, Sam told us about his girlfriend: a young woman his age with whom he had been planning a ten-day bicycle tour through France. A few days before they were due to leave she canceled the trip. She had decided to go on vacation with another guy who'd just gotten a car for his birthday.

"Did this change in plans come because of a fight?" I asked.

"No, not at all. She had said quite a few times before that she preferred traveling by car to pedaling herself around."

"So what's the problem?"

"Well, I was shocked. I asked her then if comfort was so much more important than spending time together. She told me I was being old-fashioned, and that she would have plenty of time to ride around with me in the future."

"And what did you answer her?"

"I told her that if that was how she felt, then what we had couldn't be true love. I said that there was no way she could really be in love with me. She told me I was being childish, making such a big deal about the whole thing. She said she needed a more open-minded boy-friend. I said that being 'open-minded' was not the same thing as 'true love.' Since then I've kept my distance from her."

At this point in the conversation, I noticed Vicky. She seemed to be deep in thought, then she said, as if to her-self, "Yes, right, true love."

I felt that she had hit upon an issue of her own. She continued by cutting into our discussion.

"May I ask a question?"

"Definitely," I said, "but we still owe Sam an answer."

"Sam, you said that you were shocked by your girl-friend's cancellation. You didn't expect anything like this from her?"

"No, not at all. It really came as a surprise."

"You've decided that she can't really love you, and

frankly it seems like you're right. If you are right, then you've become disillusioned. You see your relationship clearly for what it is."

"Yeah, that's pretty much the feeling I have."

"So you've freed yourself from the illusion of the relationship. You've distanced yourself from her and your illusion has changed to disappointment. Even though it might have been painful, you should be happy that you're free of this illusion."

Sam considered this.

Finally Vicky was able to get around to her question.

"Is there such a thing as true love? Sam believes that there must be. I used to believe the same thing when I was his age. Part of me still does, yet I'm becoming less and less sure, and I don't know how to find out whether I'm right or wrong.

"When I met my husband I was sure we loved each other. We really could talk to each other—it was important to us. When I asked him how he felt, he used to really open up. We were thrilled to be bringing each other so much happiness. The sexual chemistry was terrific, too. He loved to seduce me at the most unexpected times, and in the strangest places. We both felt free, and we enjoyed going a little crazy.

"As time went on he spoke less and less to me and became more and more short-tempered. I began to feel that he was just using me for his own pleasures. When he touched me—if he touched me at all—it was not out of tenderness. He only caressed me to get me hot enough to have sex with him. Around then I realized he probably had other women.

"At first I thought it was just a phase, and that it would pass. His behavior did annoy me, but I did still love him. Now I hardly see a point to our relationship. We live pretty peacefully together, but I know that love must be something more. I don't know if I'm building false expectations or if I'm doing something wrong, but I do believe in true love. I feel as if I'm standing in front of a huge cloud hoping that somewhere in the cloud I'll be able to find love. Do you know what love is?"

I felt that this question was important not to just Sam and Vicky. All the others, especially the married couples, insisted we tackle this topic first.

I usually approach difficult issues with caution, like a careful animal approaching an enemy or sneaking up on a kill. What we call love is so multifaceted, so changing and colorful—much like the view through a kaleidoscope. Some feel that love is a sexual drive. That's why the French, English, and Italians use the expression "making love." Others lavish love on their dog or on their car. Many mothers pour their love on their children and not so much on their spouse. I began explaining these ideas of love to the group and Vicky added, "There is a man in our neighborhood who lives for his football team. We have often remarked that he loves his team more than anything else."

"You're right." I continued, "A person doesn't only love objects. He can love ideas or goals. For one person, the greatest thrill—his 'love'—might be his scientific research, for another her political convictions. For these people, 'love' becomes a devotion to their personal ideals or goals."

Vicky broke in: "Am I understanding this correctly? A person can basically love *anything*? While one person is in love with her partner, another thinks just as lovingly about his hobby during his every waking moment? You could say that he's just as much in love with his ideal as another might be in love with a person. I'm not totally convinced, but I suppose I see your point: He who loves can love either a person or an object or an idea."

"I understand why you're not convinced. You're saying that we love what we often and gladly think about— be it a person or a goal or a fantasy. I see it slightly differently: *True love* is not just thinking and dreaming about something constantly; it is also devoting ourselves to and working at something without tiring."

"Of course you're right," said Vicky. "I understand

that. True love is what you do with single-minded devotion. But how do I know if what I'm doing so devotedly is love?"

I thought about that for a while and then I answered her: "A person loves that which has some kind of worth above everything else in his or her life. But a lot of people believe that they can—or want—to only love that thing which has the *highest* worth, that 'once-in-a-lifetime' kind of value. It doesn't have to be the love of God or an ideal or even your perfect mate. Consider why people do things: For many of them either desire or security are the highest values in life. That may seem matter-of-fact to you."

Vicky raised her eyebrows. "I have to say that it seems almost trivial, commonplace. Is that what love is about? Do you really believe that most people see love as something between desire and security?"

"When you put it that way, I have to say yes. But let me start from the beginning. What we do know is that people, just like every other living thing, have been procreating for millions of years. Without desire this wouldn't be possible, especially in higher-order animals. Aside from the need to procreate, human newborns need years and years of parental care. That is why the greatest needs of mother and child are protection and security. With this in mind, do you agree that in the case of procreation, desire and security are the highest values in a human's life?"

"Definitely. When you look at it from a purely biological point of view, it certainly makes sense," Vicky answered.

"Good," I said. "Let's consider people again. I think that when they talk about love they're usually referring either to desire or security. You could say that this is trivial and commonplace, almost obvious. I would prefer to call it natural. It is important to see desire and security under their many different aspects. Desire isn't just about sexual gratification. You can have a pleasurable reaction to an attractive body or appealing gestures. If a person's approach is like this, or if he just wants to reassure himself that he is sexy and attractive, then he flirts. This person is not interested in a 'possible relationship'—or an understanding and responsible friendship or bond."

"Most of the time I see it the same way," agreed Vicky. "It might be that I meet a man who appeals to me and I can picture a relationship with him, but I pretty much lose interest once I realize he's only being charming to prove to himself that he's appealing. Many people are so insecure that they feel they need to chat me up and get me into bed to make sure they mean something to me. Why is it that an otherwise charming and attractive man has to approach a woman like a rooster in a henhouse?"

"So you see," I continued, "you too recognize how nature arranges things in favor of procreation. As soon as an appropriate sexual partner comes into view, sexual interest is stimulated.

"Desire is prosaic and flirting poetic, if you will, but they are definitely related. They serve nature in the push for procreation. The flirt usually is content with coquettish play. Since, for the flirt it is really only about proving his own attractiveness, he is testing himself to see where he fits in on the attractiveness scale. We could call him a 'test flirt.' A lot of men and women have gotten into trouble when they've confused this kind of behavior with an actual sexual come-on.

"Flirting also gives you a way to measure each other's sexual talents. As long as it is understood that it's not a question of a responsible, bonding, and secure relationship, this kind of interaction is not considered binding. This kind of person remains a flirt, albeit a sexual flirt."

"Sure," said Vicky. "Flirting is definitely not love. Maybe you could call it 'partial love.' But then is true love defined by keeping yourself tied to your promise of fidelity?" she asked. "The thing is, I'm not convinced by this issue of 'fidelity'—I don't like the word. It makes me feel pressured. I want to be faithful, not even by my own free will but by my own need and desire to be so. Often the promise to be faithful is made too soon, when you're young and naive. I don't like the idea of 'fidelity' as a moral imperative. Yet I personally still can't be 'unfaithful.' "

"I agree with you, Vicky. You see that the *promise* of fidelity is the counterpart of desire. It creates a forced security. Security is the second reason for what people call love. We're not dealing with the ticklish thrill of erotic abandonment. The pressure here is for a relationship to create a reliable and stable life bond. The best example of this kind of security is marriage.

"As a person initiates the courtship that will lead to marriage, he needs to prove that he can provide material security. Some do it by offering lavish gifts during courtship, some present themselves as 'breadwinners' by flaunting their high corporate positions or their doctorates and titles—as if these gave them a stamp of approval.

"Like fidelity, security also becomes an issue of moral imperative. With the statement of fidelity 'until death do us part' you're ensuring the security of your children."

Vicky shook her head. "But that sounds so egotistical! That can't be love."

"You're right again, Vicky. You asked me what love was. We agreed that flirting was a kind of 'partial love.' Well, this pressured, conservative love is the same kind of thing—a partial love. I'm just trying to show you how many aspects of love there are. In this case we're talking about the naturally ordained love that serves procreation."

Vicky was silent. So I pressed on: "Actually, love has an even more egotistical side, which you also know. That is *dominating love*. One partner dominates the other, who accepts the authoritarian behavior. Some people might even 'need' a dominating partner because they believe that strength and authority are synonymous with security."

"Yes, I see that often—that the partner with the greater sense of self dominates the other, and the submissive partner lets it happen. But how does it happen? Why does one person want power over another? Power and love are opposites. Why would you seek power instead of love?"

"Because many people want to protect themselves against the feeling of helplessness. All of us feel insecure to varying degrees with our position in life. Some people feel constantly insecure, some feel insecure about certain things at certain times, while others feel that in order to overcome their insecurities they must gain power and security at the expense of others. Power brings a feeling of strength and security that is made even stronger through material ownership."

Vicky nodded. You could tell by looking at her that a dozen such relationships were running through her mind. "I do know a few couples whose relationships come across more like battles. In the desire for power one partner tries to provoke the other, to expose him, to cut him down.

"Unfortunately, I've seen many of these kinds of marriages around me. Many of them stay together for the sake of the children or because a divorce is just too expensive. I look at them and see how resigned they are when love just isn't part of the picture anymore."

"You know, Vicky, most relationships start out with a battle for power. Just like the animals before they pair off. Men use the power of self-promotion and seduction to their advantage. The virgin and the tease use the power of their sexuality—so they can reel their fish in when he's thrashed around enough.

"Strength and power are symbols of security. Security—just like desire—is necessary by nature for procreation. In this sense we have to approach desire and security as biologically ordained parts of 'natural love.'

"When the security of a relationship is threatened by a rival, then jealousy breaks out. Then the power of love turns into the power of hate."

Cut out each of the cards above and use them to determine
your Romantic Type Chart following the instructions in
"Evaluating Your Colors of Love," page 5.

ROMANTIC TYPE
CARD 2

ROMANTIC TYPE
CARD 1

ROMANTIC TYPE
CARD 4

ROMANTIC TYPE
CARD 3

JEALOUSY

Jealousy is a topic I'm interested in," Vicky responded. "Is jealousy truly a sign of love? There are a lot of people who try to make their partners jealous on purpose, to bind them closer to themselves somehow. Is jealousy a part of love?"

"Is war a part of being a person? What frequently happens isn't necessarily normal," I told the group.

"Before we go on I want to clear up an issue. The loss of a partner doesn't necessarily need to create jealousy. When a partner dies, for example, we don't usually take it as an affront. In my book *The Laws of Harmony Within Us* I gave an unforgettable example of jealousy in a person whose spouse has died. I'm going to repeat verbatim the words of Gloria, the woman in question:

" 'I want to tell you why I came to see you. My husband is dead. I pushed him to suicide. He just couldn't take my nagging anymore, so he hanged himself in the garage. It's my fault. I murdered him. He was retired—we had our house with a nice garden. These were supposed to be our golden years, to enjoy our peace and quiet and our garden—and he's gone and left me alone. What a mean thing to do! So now he's left me sitting here all by myself.'

"Gloria, who had constantly pressured her husband with groundless jealousy, was still jealous. She was jealous of the fact that he was 'allowed' to be dead while she had to continue on her own.

"When a partner leaves us to be with someone else, we're disappointed, but I don't want to confuse disappointment with jealousy.

"In this situation, a person with no self-esteem feels offended, her pride has been wounded. Feeling offended and even wounded is understandable, but there still is no excuse for jealousy.

"I define jealousy as the groundless fear that a partner is interested in or in love with someone else. This jealousy is a result of insecurity, which in turn is a result of low self-esteem.

"Jealousy comes about when *one* partner feels she has some sort of claim over the other, that she needs to 'own' the other person. In this case she is right to feel insecure, because her claim is as unrealistic as it is unfair. You can't own another person, so she is right in believing something is amiss. If, on top of that, a partner is personally insecure, then jealousy is an unavoidable result. Through her own unfounded insecurities, the jealous person constantly fears that her relationship is being threatened. This person fears that she will lose meaning in her partner's eyes or that she has already lost her partner's interest. She feels threatened and helpless. But the jealous partner doesn't react to this threat with resignation. Instead, she fights these feelings of resignation, powerlessness, and loss with aggressive behaviors, with reproaches and accusations. So the useless and destructive Ping-Pong game of mutual accusations becomes a struggle for power. But love doesn't let itself be pressured by any kind of force. Quite the contrary: Love and power are polar opposites."

Vicky suddenly spoke up: "I'm totally convinced by what you say. Either you like someone and you grow closer to them or the whole thing is a useless sham. Love doesn't respond to force. Love doesn't have anything to do with power."

"No, exactly as I said," I continued. "It's true that love and power are polar opposites. But this might surprise you: They belong together in their polarity, just like the opposite poles of a magnet. They form a unit. This is how I see it: With true love one feels strong and secure, and in this sense powerful. So one doesn't feel any need to assert one's power over one's partner. Any kind of power play is destructive to true love.

"If we're talking about 'being in love' and the feeling of having a claim over a partner and the need to be loved by this person, then that's another story. In these cases one doesn't feel strength and security as coming from within, but as something one needs to get by exerting power over one's partner."

Charles broke in: "But it doesn't necessarily have to be that way when you're in love. Later there are definitely open or even subtle power plays, but not at first. When you first fall in love, you'll do anything to keep that feeling going."

"I'm not arguing with that, but when you're in love, you still want your partner to be thrilled and fascinated by you. You want the person you love to desire you. This is the kind of power you want to have over that person. All the ways you try to make yourself attractive are in order to win this person. As soon as the person has been won over, you have established your power over him or her. There are a lot of relationships that are based on one partner's ability to excite the other sexually, to have that kind of power over the other."

Vicky seemed to agree with this. "That makes sense to me. I can certainly imagine that you can experience a sense of power when you impress someone else. But you still haven't explained why you would make a partner jealous on purpose. Why do so many people believe that jealousy is a part of love? I just don't see it."

I tried to explain the connection as follows: "When you fall in love you're assured of having—through your partner—what you've been missing until now. This thrilling feeling that you finally have everything for your world to be perfect is a kind of security, a feeling of power. The happiness of being in love makes us feel secure and protected from all wants and dangers.

"With true love a person feels strong and secure as an individual. Being in love, on the other hand, doesn't make you stronger as an individual. You get all of your feelings of security from your partner.

"Unfortunately, the minute you feel you've lost your power of attraction—hence whatever power you had over your partner—you fall back into the condition of insecurity and lacking you started out with. Jealousy is a fight against this falling back, against helplessness and confusion. People sometimes begin to believe that if you want to possess someone you have to care lovingly for your possession. Unfortunately for them, this is a miscalculation. A jealous person might try to pamper his partner with a medley of attentions, to buy the other's affections—

but this is not loving care. Actually, it's an unfair ploy to make the other person dependent, thus dominating and possessing him or her."

Vicky shook her head. "Dominating love is still a kind of partial love, like flirting and conservative love. It feeds on itself." She continued, "When I say love, I mean something totally different. The problem is that I can't exactly say what I mean. It must be a feeling similar to what you experience when you're in love, maybe not quite so giddy. It needs to have a stronger, more lasting, basis."

FALLING IN LOVE

I grinned, because love is a delicious topic both in reality and in discussion. I began, "Falling is a fascinating feeling. It's true that falling in love can open the doors to the poetry of life. Unfortunately, too many people only end up peering through the keyhole. Some think *being in love* is *true love*. Unfortunately, when the excitement of falling in love is over, many people tend to just look for a new partner who can fulfill their ideal better than the last one. In order to experience these giddy feelings of love, they use and misuse a new victim each time, a person who they believe will fulfill all of their ardent desires and illusions. The lyrics to love songs and popular music give these people their directions in love."

Charles seemed pretty displeased with my attack on the notion of falling in love: "I don't agree with you at all. There is still a kind of love that hits you over the head and you feel that it's mutual. That's the feeling I've always yearned for. I mean that this feeling grips you with a kind of inner excitement, because suddenly you realize that the person in front of you has all the qualities you've been searching for."

"I know what you mean: love at first sight that is, at the same time, true love," I offered.

"That's exactly what I was trying to say. It *has* to exist," Charles answered.

I pressed him further. "Is this how you came across real, true love? Did you have this kind of experience?"

"No, actually an affection developed between me and my girlfriend, and developed into a deep bond. It seems to us that it has since grown and grown. I do want to say that it has usually been the difficult times, the tough situations, that have brought us closer and closer."

"So your idea of instant, thunderstruck love at first sight developing into true love is just that—a dream. You yourself have not experienced this.

"I do want to start off by explaining what I mean. Falling in love, romanticism, the giddy affection that you hear about in love songs and read about in romance novels and that is glorified in magazines, is just an image of longing. You could compare it to the scores of bewitching melodies. These images of love are really only the notes, not quite music. You have to make your own music, just as you have to nurture true love on your own.

"It is not a given that you have all the right 'notes' for love. It's sometimes easy to fall in love with another person if you've got the wrong notes. These 'wrong notes' are often superficial and contrived, and are particularly attractive to you when you are trying to fulfill a misguided longing.

"These 'wrong notes' are usually visual, looks, the whole body from head to toe, hair, eyes, mouth, chest, hands, buttocks, and legs. What we often first notice is something as superficial as clothing. What is more important, though, is the expression of a person, their movements and how they carry themselves, that we experience as attraction. When these signals match up with our expectations, this is, for many people, reason enough to fall in love. The doors are thrown open to anyone who seems to promise desire or security. This is the reaction we were describing as 'natural love.'

"For people to whom spiritual values are important, a feeling that another person matches their ideals and shares their values becomes the idea that 'Wow, we're on the same wavelength!' Personality—which is multifaceted and difficult to pin down—interests, and intelligence also become part of the equation. When these characteristics also seem to match up, then a person can believe that not only has she fallen in love, but that she's found true love itself. But true love can be elusive, even in a relationship with the most auspicious beginnings. It doesn't just come; you have to shape it yourself.

"By falling in love you can hold down your loneliness and your inability to truly love, but only for a short time. To break out of this vicious circle of falling in love and getting hurt, of wrecked relationships, and to find true love, you have to turn yourself around. You have to change the way you approach things from the backstepping of illusory expectations into the forward march of true love."

Charles still held on to his ideas. "But I would like to know why with certain people—even if you've only just met them—you feel this overwhelming feeling that this is the one, the one I've been looking for. What creates this exciting, stirring fascination?"

MAGNETISM AND ATTRACTION

I answered Charles. "Earlier when I was referring to the general reasons for attraction, I was trying to show that that kind of fascination can only be the overture to true love. I don't want to avoid your question—it's a fascinating topic in and of itself.

"As you sit at a café or anywhere where you can observe people, there are calculations going on inside your head—or heart. With lightning speed you judge anyone who comes into view. Are they interesting and attractive or boring and nothing to write home about? Sometimes your calculations just stop. Lightning has hit and your feelings are kindled. Fascination sweeps you away. Now, how and why does this come about? Can we discover the secret?

"I want to share with you two experiences that could be the key for our understanding. I was still a young therapist when a twenty-three-year-old woman came to see me. She was absolutely crazy about a man even though he wasn't terribly interested in her. When I heard that he was her dream partner because he had her three ideal qualities—black hair, thin build, and a tall frame—I had to ask her, 'So why else do you love him?'

" 'I don't know, I hardly know him,' was her answer.

"This conversation made a deep impression on me. Before that I had never imagined that you could fall so deeply in love based on so little.

"Here's an example of the opposite situation. A very attractive, sensible, and intelligent student of mine had her eye on a fellow student who was probably the epitome of male attractiveness. She thought he might finally be a man with whom she could fall in love. Being attractive herself, it didn't take too long before he asked her out for dinner. This seemed to be a good sign, pointing toward a burgeoning love story; however, quite the opposite happened. Even though the man was attractive and intelligent, the relationship just didn't pan out. All the signs were good, but somehow 'love' never happened. What had blocked it?

"What made that young woman fall in love in the first example? What held love back in the second?

"There are actually two completely different reasons for deep attraction or falling in love. The first reason is easy to explain. It is based on outward appearances. Body type, clothing, and hair are exactly of this kind of outward signal.

"The second cause for attraction is not outwardly visible. It isn't a quality you can photograph. It is what we mean when we talk about someone's personality. We experience each person as a characteristic personality. What we sense from a person is more or less her psychological and emotional state, as well as her unique qualities and ways of thinking. We'll call it a person's nature.

"You can't see a person's nature, but you can experience it and understand it intuitively. We feel it and understand it on the basis of millions of little impressions. These impressions pass in the blink of an eye, but we take them in and incorporate them almost unconsciously. They can be as subtle as a movement, a twitch of the lips, the flicker of an eyelash. We recognize the nature of a person based more on *how* she says something than *what* she actually says.

"We are able to intuit these signals in a person when we connect with her and because, in her, we recognize parts of our own nature. This is why we can size up a person just a few moments after meeting her without realizing why we have a particular reaction, or even without being able to verbalize our feelings. Just like we can recognize a familiar melody after just a few notes, we can sometimes feel out the nature of another person quickly and accurately.

"So falling in love can be a product of outer—and in this case mostly erotic—signals. It can also be a product of our understanding and connecting with a person's nature. Based on this understanding we make a split-second decision on the person's suitability as a partner."

Michael spoke up. "That's exactly what I think. It often happens that I am attracted to a woman, and it's pretty understandable that I might fall in love with her. I admit that part of the attraction is the idea of being able to show off a beautiful woman on my arm. But is it so surprising to fall in love with her?"

"That is exactly our question: Under which conditions do we fall in love? Does our potential partner have to be sexy, or successful, rich, or even grasping and needy? Once we've answered these questions, it won't be surprising at all that you do or don't fall in love with that particular person.

"I've said before that when outer signals or a person's nature somehow connect with us, then we fall in love with him. We want to talk about what those signs are exactly. Before we do, we have to clear up exactly what we mean by the word *expectations* in relation to the process of falling in love.

"When you *expect* something, that means you are

waiting for something to happen that you've experienced before. Naturally you expect the night to follow the day, to be rewarded for a task you've carried out, or to pay a given price for a product.

"The expectations we have of love are completely different. You don't wait for the same thing to happen to you that has happened a thousand times before. Quite the opposite: You expect to find whatever it is that you've been looking and hoping for for a long time, but you haven't yet found. In order to fall in love, you expect what has never happened before.

"So the expectations of love are the complete opposite of real experiences. Often they are fantasy situations or the most ardently desired ideals.

"These expectations, which are driving desires and wishes, come from a single motive. Their cause is some kind of deficit, a fault. Every deficit we feel in ourselves wakes a desire to overcome it. A thirsty person wishes for nothing more strongly than to drink.

"What happens in love can be compared to a horseshoe magnet. One pole is negative and the opposite pole is positive. The negative pole stands for the deficit or fault. The positive pole can be compared to desires and wishes. There is a magnetic field between these two poles. The metal that comes into this field will be drawn in with great strength and will be held between the two poles.

"The same kind of incredible strength we find between the two poles of the magnet is found in our model of love. It's the energy transfer between the 'deficit pole' and its opposite pole, which is the longed-for power of attractiveness that no mere mortal could withstand."

Julie laughed. "I've envisioned it that way when I've been hit by the proverbial lightning bolt. Is there a conductor for this lightning or is passion a hit-or-miss situation? I would think you'd need to know what your fatal flaw is before this kind of magnetic reaction can take place."

"Again, that's our question," I continued. "Where does this love deficit come from? Why does the desire for a happy and loving partnership remain unfulfilled for most people? Many people actually experience an inner sense of loneliness—even if they're living with a partner. They long for a person with whom a full and loving relationship is possible. The deficit of loving relationships is not the result of a lack of opportunities but a result of people's inability to take these opportunities. A personal reticence is at fault that comes from a fear of rejection, or simple insecurity, dependence, fragility, or even the fear of not being attractive enough.

"Even though these are mostly imagined shortcomings, they manage to wreck a lot of people's lives. In order to free ourselves of these feelings we gravitate toward people who have everything we believe we lack and more. If you don't think you're very attractive, or think you're not very interesting to others, then you're likely to fall in love with someone who is that much more attractive and interesting."

Charles broke in, "Don't you think that's changed? I mean these days we discuss sex pretty openly. We discuss orgasms with the same ease as dental hygiene."

I answered him. "There's as big a difference between saying and doing as there is between a map of Paris and the actual city. I find that despite all the erotic liberties we take in conversation, people are still insecure and uncomfortable with an actual erotic situation. This is mostly because in those situations we're not dealing in words and images but in the real act of bringing our own personality positively across to another person. Because of these insecurities of personality most people's spontaneity is also blocked.

"Every time we suppress an attraction because of an insecurity we strengthen our erotic 'blocks' and therefore our deficits.

"These blocks create a lasting deficit. That's why many people fall in love with sexually attractive partners who represent the desired erotic fulfillment. Some fall in love with partners who give the appearance of security and safety. Others fall in love because their partner is fun, spontaneous, and easy to be with—these qualities somehow compensate for their own insecurities. Others still fall for their partner's social prominence or wealth. Whatever flaw compensation a potential partner offers is enough to make us fall in love.

"In all of these cases we look for the compensation of our own flaws. The problem with this behavior is that we tend to end up with partners who are our polar opposites. If you feel insignificant, you'll go for a powerful person. If you feel lonely, you'll go for a dependent partner who'll give you the sense of security you need. If you feel insecure, you'll let yourself be won over by a self-confident partner. If you're trying to compensate for your own shortcomings through your partner, you're only jumping out of the frying pan and into the fire. These relationships never deliver the blissful happiness we think they promise.

"If you want to be made complete through your partner, you won't succeed—even though the feeling of being in love gives you the impression of wholeness. You have to get this all-important sense of completeness by yourself—only then will you be ready for true love."

Charles looked as if I had attacked him personally. "That's just great. You're making falling in love into something miserable!"

"I'm not trying to put anything down. Falling in love is primarily the basis for the natural love we described earlier. Secondly it opens up a world of well-being and happiness, and it even gives some people a creative push. Please understand that I am not condemning 'falling in love,' I'm just defining it. The definitions of the expectations of love and their causes should make things clearer for us. They should open our eyes to the fact that being in love and true love are two radically different things. It's not what novels, love songs, and movies portray in a short-sighted way. The causes of falling in love and the bases for true love are completely different."

Julie wanted to clarify the point. "Okay, so I get the difference. Now that you point it out, I can see that so many of the relationships that start out so gloriously end badly, sometimes even painfully. I can understand that falling in love leads to false expectations and desires that, sooner or later—usually in the first three months of marriage—end up being unfulfilled."

I tried to put Julie's words into an image. "I see it like this: When two people fall in love, the lines of their lives cross. The magnet has worked its power over the negative-deficit pole of one partner and the positive, desired pole of the other and brought them together.

"By making this connection, we do temporarily fill up whatever part of us is empty. We're either sexually contented or materially secure. Yet living together changes people. Each of us becomes someone slightly different from who we were before we met our partner. Because each new situation changes us, it's inevitable that the lines that once crossed will separate again—unless they were running parallel to begin with. In earlier times interest in desire and security was enough to create and maintain a partnership. Today things are different, primarily because society has given men and women so many more 'acceptable' options to marriage and family. Yet these options have less to do with sex, money, and social prestige than with what we can demand emotionally.

"When the emotional needs aren't being completely met, the life lines of the couple separate after a few years of marriage. In these cases the couple decides to break up or they just plow on resignedly."

Julie continued, "I can see now that saving the relationship is not a matter of spicing up your sex life or trying to recapture the feeling you had when you first fell in love. It always seemed strange to me that you could recapture love through sexy lingerie or a weekend getaway or through role playing. It seems to me that we need to graduate from falling in love to true love. We have to stop going backwards with illusionary expectations and go forward into true love."

"Exactly!" I agreed. "We shouldn't be trying for a second chance at first love. Instead we should be shooting for a new kind of relationship, namely the stability of true love."

THE BASICS OF ATTRACTION

I haven't asked my question yet," began Julie. "What are the causes for falling in love? But more important, are there specific types of people to whom we react better as potential partners? I have seen an interesting pattern with my friends. When I see a particular type of man I can tell you which one of my friends will go for him."

"That's exactly what I had in mind. We want to find and learn to recognize the reasons you're talking about. In your words, we want to figure out for what reason we go for one person rather than another.

"I want to give you an interesting example that I was able to observe firsthand. Some time ago I had an attractive twenty-two-year-old secretary working for me. She was very reliable and friendly, but unfortunately she had weak self-esteem. A handsome young lawyer started hanging around her. His particular deficit arose from a lack of attention and love from his divorced mother. He had always had the feeling he was in her way as she pursued one after another in a string of boyfriends. Because of this lack of affection he had a tendency to attach himself to his partners in a most unhealthy way. This led to a pattern of submissive loving. In the particular case of my secretary he went so far as to drive her to a nearby city to see a musician she had fallen in love with perform. Unfortunately this labor of love had the opposite effect from what he desired. Instead of thankfulness and love, he earned his place in her affections as chauffeur and wimp.

"This secretary went on to meet a man whom she believed she should marry. She was impressed by his secure and self-possessed attitude. He played this role well as the independent son of a wealthy industrialist. What had at first come across as attractive self-possession mutated into authoritarian dictatorship once they were married. Even sexually he was incapable of tenderness. He would often take his wife by surprise and attempt to rape her. At first he succeeded in his violent pursuits, as she was too exhausted to defend herself. These incidents were both painful and demoralizing for her.

"Why had these two fallen for each other? Why had she not responded to the loving attentions of her first suitor? This particular example shows us once again the structure of falling in love. The woman's deficit was weak self-esteem. Because of this she played right into the hands of her dominating partner.

"One lovely summer night the woman suggested to her husband that they take a little walk. He wanted to know what for. She was too embarrassed to say that she wanted to enjoy the feeling of that evening, so she blurted, 'To see the moon.'

" 'That's ridiculous, haven't you ever seen the moon before?' was his dispassionate answer. His deficits were his inability to understand the feelings of his partner, his incapacity for loving understanding, his lack of tenderness, and his inability to form bonds. All of this was the result of many rejections from secure, independent women in his past. Because of these experiences he specifically needed and sought out partners who were insecure and easily governed. Only with such a partner could he get away with his sadistic sexual practices. He could only manipulate an insecure woman as a sexual object. He had no other way of relating to women. As a businessman he took advantage of his outwardly secure no-nonsense attitude, but in terms of sexuality these attitudes translated into a need for empty encounters and sexual—often violent—conquest."

Julie had a question. "When we talk about erotic love relationships, do we all have the same thing in mind?"

Charlie answered her. "I think that what most people

have in mind is pretty much the same, but when it comes down to what people actually *do*, then that's a whole different story."

I asked the rest of the group what they thought. Some were hesitant to give an opinion at first, but they all finally agreed that the concept of an erotic love relationship is roughly the same for everyone.

"I'm interested to see that you all believe this. I used to believe it too, but I have since realized that not all people have the same understanding of erotic love relationships. I realized my error through the results of extensive research that I've been conducting over the past five years. I based this research on four colors. These colors were carefully selected and completely different, for example an exciting orange-red or a calming dark purple. In the course of my research I always asked the same questions: How do you experience your erotic love relationships? Which of these colors best matches your experience? Second best? The least?

"Just yesterday I ran the test on a stuntwoman, whose job requires her to simulate car accidents and all sorts of dangerous situations. She found that orange-red best exemplified her idea of the erotic; the deep purple left her cold. On the other hand, her director related erotic love experiences with the deep purple but couldn't relate at all to the orange-red.

"With just four colors we are able to distinguish twenty-four ways of experiencing erotic love relationships. Most people are astonished to see that you can perceive how one experiences an erotic love relationship so easily.

"This research has shown that people have completely different perceptions of something we all use the same name for. If we happen to have matching perceptions, it has more to do with subtle similarities between people than with the universality of the concept."

Julie was insistent. "I understand that falling in love is a way to free ourselves from an otherwise unsatisfactory life situation or, as you say, a compensation for an emotional deficit. But you still haven't answered my second question. Is there a particular type to which other particular types react in a specific way? From the examples you've given, we can see that this kind of matching up seems to occur. As I've said before, I have experienced it with my own friends and the men they go for."

I agreed with Julie that there were indeed certain types and relationships that could be named. I elaborated, "Outward appearances, such as blond hair, big breasts, long legs, tight buttocks, or a man's hairy chest, can work as signals of attraction. I do believe, however, that most of the time what we really fall for are the personal and emotional characteristics of a person. If we start with the idea that we fall in love to fulfill some kind of expectation, which in turn is a product of our own deficits, then we have to ask ourselves which kind of deficits and privations occur most often. From this we can decide which expectations are the most common to those who are falling in love. I am of the opinion that there are basic types of relationships that constitute 'falling in love,' which we can distinguish and name.

"Every basic type has a different deficit and therefore a particular way of or reason for falling for someone. I want to give two quick examples here, after which I'll go over the basic types in more detail.

"Example One: The person who experienced suppression in the parental home, or who feels pressured by the circumstances of life, wants to escape from these situations. This person is then likely to fall in love with a person who seems to live his life unfettered by convention. This person believes she can fulfill her dream of freedom and carefree existence with this partner.

"Example Two: The person whose family situation was broken up by divorce or illness or frequent relocation may feel constantly insecure. This person is most likely to fall in love with someone who offers him a sense of security and stability.

"These two basic needs affect most of the causes and types of falling in love. On the one hand we have the desire for sexual fulfillment, and on the other, material security. We've noted that both of these are parts of 'natural love.' Sexual desire and material security are basic needs for both men and women. These needs must somehow be fulfilled. They can be expressed as either a requirement or as a problem or deficit in a person. For most men sexual fulfillment plays a particularly large role. Material security, on the other hand, is a far more important expectation for many women. Some people satisfy their need for material security through luxury—they won't be happy until they're drinking champagne out of golden goblets and shopping in designer stores.

"Outside of these two basic needs there are other deficits and expectations that cause us to fall in love. After sexual desire and material security, social prestige presents itself as a third conductor for love. If socially you feel like an insignificant little gray mouse or if you're an insatiable show-off, then you're likely to be very impressed by someone who has standing in the community or has some degree of fame. How your potential mate gained his standing is often irrelevant. It could be through a career, or money, or even because of a scandal. People who constantly need to feel worthy have a predilection for, and easily fall in love with, those they deem to be important or prominent in society."

Vicky spoke up. "That may well be the case for many people. They might fall in love because of one, two, or even all three of the reasons you've discussed, but I can't help feeling that there are other reasons. In fact, I'm sure that there are certain feelings that wake an excitement in people and lead them to fall in love. I once fell instantly in love with a man because he had such twinkling eyes and he laughed so heartily. I felt he had to be a happy and open-minded person. I wasn't wrong about that. Unfortunately, he was also unreliable, and it had never crossed his mind to work hard at making a living."

"You're right, Vicky. I also believe that sensitive people fall in love mostly because of the feelings or intuitions you describe. I actually find these feelings and intuitions more interesting reasons for love than sex, material security, and prestige.

"May I ask you, Vicky, what your life was like when you fell in love with Mr. Happiness?"

"Sure. I had just started working in publishing, and my boss at the time was rather unpleasant. At first he was really friendly; he often asked me out to dinner. Soon I realized that he was actually interested in me even though he was a married man. I decided I should distance myself. He took it pretty badly, and after that he was always grumpy and he bitched about me to everyone. I would have quit if I could have afforded it. Unfortunately, I was pretty strapped financially at the time . . . oh, I get it! What I was missing at that time was cheerfulness. That was my deficit. Now I understand why I was so attracted to this happy man."

Julie had her own example. "When I was a student I fell in love with a classmate because he was such an intellectual. I was really impressed by all of his deep ideas and his breadth of knowledge. I never imagined being able to have such knowledge myself."

Some of us smiled. I asked her, "So have you figured out what your negative magnetic pole was? Your deficit was your belief that you weren't good enough. You wanted to be just as intelligent as he was, and to have all of his knowledge. Do you see that your classmate was the positive pole to your negative?"

"Yes, that must have been it, because outside of the fascinating discussions we had, the sexual element of the relationship was lousy."

I continued, "We still haven't isolated one of the most important reasons for attraction. It is possibly the most elusive, but also the strongest. It is the attraction of resonance. You don't know why, but when you meet a person you have the feeling that you're on their same wavelength. You sense this resonance without being able to really put your finger on it. It's not visual and you can't rationalize it. Just by talking to this person you sense it as a resonance of feelings and ideas; by making contact you experience it as a sensual resonance. The sensual, erotic resonance can be sensed with something as simple as the first handshake.

"The resonance of feelings is sensed in conversation. However, it has less to do with the topic of discussion than with the way the person expresses herself. The way she listens, how understanding and attentive she is, and, above all, how she answers your questions determine how you perceive this resonance. When you get a feeling of genuine trust, then your resonance is on the same wavelength. Only a mature person is able to reach this stage. Without a sense of personal freedom, without security, and without solid self-esteem, this kind of connection is impossible. This is probably why it happens so rarely— yet almost all of us wish for it. Because this connection is so rare yet so coveted, we find ourselves almost perpetually ready and willing to fall in love. In this case the negative pole isn't looking for an illusionary complement; rather, we're reaching for a real relationship."

TRUE LOVE

As you can see, *love* is a word we use to denote all kinds of relationships. Most of the time it has to do with the need for desire and security. That's why we often use the word *love* as a euphemism for egotistical goals."

"That can't be the whole story," Vicky piped up. She had been listening with an obviously growing sense of unease. "Romantic love is just another kind of partial love, much like flirting, the conservative love, and the dominant love we've discussed.

"My cloud of unknowing has become unpleasantly clearer, but I still feel that love—in which I believe—is still hidden in there somewhere."

"I understand where you're coming from," I assured her. "I just wanted to show in how many ways and also how inaccurately we use the word *love*.

"I'm not trying to say that everyone who's looking for love is looking for desire or material security.

"The *complete* love, which I believe to be true love, is found very rarely. Even the books and novels that talk about love so often rarely refer to this kind of true love."

Vicky was growing impatient. "So how do I find it? How can I look for true love?"

"There's your mistake, Vicky—you're *looking* for love. The point is that you can't find true love ready-made; you have to nurture and develop it yourself. Even when you've fulfilled all kinds of expectations, love is not paradise. It's not a place where you and your partner can cavort like Adam and Eve, enjoying all the pleasures, comforts, and securities of your relationship. Love is not the promised land where fruits blossom on your tongue and Lady Luck watches over you. True love is a garden where feelings of understanding, unity, attention, helpfulness, respect, and responsibility must be sown before they are reaped. Once you've sown these seeds, then you can nurture and encourage them to blossom and grow—eventually you'll be able to reap them.

"Love is not the same thing as being in love. It's something you can reach only if the both of you respectfully strive for harmony. If you're not ready for it, if you need to be loved more than you are ready to love, or if you're looking for security, you're heading for disaster before you even begin. By indulging in these expectations you are programmed to fail.

"As long as your past disappointments haven't made you bitter or resigned, you will still yearn for the feeling of being in love.

"True love, the kind that brings fulfillment and happiness, is something totally different from simply 'being in love.' True love is complete love."

Vicky's expression of unease changed to one of expectation. She asked, "What is this complete love? That's exactly what I've been missing in my life. Flirting, conservative love, dominating love, and romantic love—those are all partial loves. What is this complete love I'm looking for?"

"Good," I said. "Complete love encompasses two basic issues that at first may seem contradictory. The first one, which you may have already gotten a sense of, is erotic unity. Namely the care you take to achieve physical, emotional, and spiritual unity. In this state of unity you want to conquer your partner and at the same time give yourself over completely. You want both things: to give and to take. Without a tender, lingering devotion, this kind of unity is impossible. Erotic unity is not expressed only in the sexual aspect of the relationship; it also comes across in your readiness to understand and connect with your partner on an emotional and spiritual level."

Without giving me a chance to finish, Vicky wanted

to get to the heart of the discussion. "That makes complete sense to me. We all want that. But why do most people fail to achieve this fulfilling, lasting sense of unity? Or even if they do, why can't they make it last? Why do so many relationships just fall apart? This is what interests me the most."

"I don't think I can give you a simple answer. I hope that you'll understand, even if at first it doesn't make sense. There is a second part of complete love: respect for your partner. Let me say it a little more clearly: In order to achieve full love you must learn to respect the individuality and independence of your partner. This means nothing more than giving your partner the freedom to live as his or her inner convictions demand. You have to treasure the fact that he or she lives this way, as his or her inner sense of freedom and self-respect require.

"When you truly love your partner's individuality, then you can also respect the fact that your partner will change. I want to call this second basic issue respectful love.

"Erotic unity and respectful love are the two opposites that become complete in a fulfilling love relationship. On the one hand, you have the erotic love, which strives for understanding and unity, and on the other hand, respectful love, which requires the respect of your partner's individuality and changing nature.

"Love that is capable of embracing these two opposites can develop into warm-hearted, fulfilling love. This kind of love brings trust and confidence, frees our creative energies, and engenders tolerance and benevolence. Complete love is the basis for a life filled with happiness."

"Now I feel it. That was a set of blinders I had put on myself. I thought that in love I had to give up my individuality to really unite with my partner. I'm not even sure I've completely grasped the concept. I still have a lot to work out before I can get rid of these blinders and my negative attitudes and habits. Even so the cloud has retreated—no, better yet, it's disappeared."

I was silent. You could see the relaxation and peace spreading over her features.

After a moment Vicky spoke again, almost to herself, in a warm, soft voice. "Yes, that's love, that's true love."

I let a few more moments pass before I suggested we break for lunch.

During our break we enjoyed the delicious gourmet food and the beautiful view of the glimmering, silver lake crowned by mountains whose snowy caps glistened in the sun.

Once we were all together again Julie opened up the discussion. "This morning we talked about true love. It made me think of a saying we often hear: In order to love another you must first love yourself. Am I getting it right?"

I answered her. "I have never felt comfortable with that saying. You could take loving yourself to mean that you constantly need to make yourself comfortable, to gratify and reward yourself or even to spoil yourself like a child. If you look at it this way, then that saying is not only wrong, it can be damaging. To love oneself is fine, as long as we're talking about having a sincere, trustworthy, and sensible picture of ourselves. Perhaps I can say it more clearly: Loving myself has to mean that I cultivate and take care of my self-esteem and my self-trust. That means, first, that in all situations I treat things the same way I would want to be treated. Second, in order to maintain trust in myself, I must always work toward my goals. As an example: Think of how much practice it took you to drive a car with complete security and understanding.

"The sentence 'I must love myself before I can love another' can also be taken to mean 'I must be able to take care of myself, I must trust in my abilities to do what I believe is right.' The person who fulfills these requirements is sure of himself and capable of true love.

"On the other hand, a person who is insecure can quickly become jealous. It's impossible to have a sincere and harmonious relationship with a jealous person. She will always feel like she's being taken for granted and isn't getting enough love. Because of this she will always feel a lack of consideration on the part of her partner. If a person feels worthless, she has a tendency to blame it on others. This leads insecure people to believe that they are actually being oppressed.

"A person who feels worthless or insecure is not ready to acknowledge her partner. She feels that if she loves someone the other person should make her a priority. By doing so she creates an even greater disproportion between herself and her partner—she makes herself feel even less worthy. Despite this prioritization of the partner, the insecure person needs boundless attention, acknowledgment, and support."

Julie added, "I know a few people who through their great gestures and general showing off give the impression of being quite sure of themselves. Can I assume that these people are actually quite insecure?"

"That is a very important conclusion. Any exaggeration, be it arrogance or great shows of modesty, is grounded in quite the opposite of what it appears. Anyone who acts overbearing, complacent, or arrogant is merely overcompensating for their insecurity.

"It is valuable to be able to recognize that the overbearing person is trying above all to overcome his own sense of lack or insecurity. It's also a good idea to understand that his contemptuous behavior toward another person is a way for him to somehow diminish the other. This is his way of alleviating the enormous sense of worthlessness he carries with him.

"We see a lot of this kind of arrogant behavior toward women by men who are insecure. Unfortunately for them, in a real partnership there must be a sense of equality."

"*Equality,* there's a good word!" Julie exclaimed. Michael looked at her and raised his eyebrows. We all laughed at this mute exchange.

Michael felt that he was under fire, so he started in on a defense that was as weak as it was short: "I think that's asking too much!"

"So do you believe that men and women are equal?" I asked provocatively.

"Well, there is a significant difference between men and women," he countered.

I shot back, "I didn't say that men and women are the same, I simply said that they have the same worth."

"I guess," murmured Michael.

Once again Vicky spoke up. "When only those people who work on their self-esteem and have a strong belief in themselves can truly fall in love, then it doesn't surprise me that so few people have the ability to love truly. How can you tell if a person has high self-esteem and believes in himself?"

I turned the question over to the group. "How does a

person feel when he can respect himself because he pursues his convictions and believes in himself enough to do so?"

The suggested feelings were "competent," "authoritative," "strong sense of personality," "respected."

"No, that's how others evaluate him or her. How does a person feel *inside*?"

Once again Julie had an answer: "She feels secure. When someone believes in herself and is self-assured, she has achieved a sense of personal security."

"Thanks for hitting the nail on the head, Julie," I concurred.

Vicky also wanted to give her opinion. "So you find out if someone is capable of true love by seeing if he has that sense of personal security. That is to say, once you get beyond how most people pretend they're secure, you find that there are only a few people, usually the ones who are naturally modest, who are really secure enough to be capable of true love."

"Thank you, Vicky. You've got it exactly. You have come upon an important criterion for a good partnership.

"Naturally we aren't all born with these qualities. They come about through daily living. It's important that we be honest with ourselves on a daily basis in order to steer ourselves into harmony. True love is an art form that can be learned. Unfortunately, most people don't know the prerequisites. They think that pretty words and presents will do the trick."

Next, Charles wanted to know if you could only love one person, or if it was possible to truly love more than one person at a time. I never answer that kind of question immediately; I try to let the group put in their own feelings and ideas before I speak.

Vicky was convinced that true love was only possible with one partner. Michael thought that you could honestly love more than one person. Julie and the others felt that the love of one's children or parents or even friends could be true love.

At this point I broke in. "We agreed earlier that a person loves what he or she holds to be of primary, uppermost worth. These two qualities—'worthy' and 'primary and uppermost'—can be related to different aspects of life. If you have two lovers, you can't say you have a primary, uppermost love for each of them. You could say that you love one partner in one way, and the other in another way. You certainly like both of them, but neither of them is of uppermost value.

"I'm saying that Vicky is right when she says that you can only truly love one person. We're both saying that if, when you see the words 'love you' with sincere conviction, you are experiencing that sense of uppermost worth.

"That doesn't mean that we can't find other people

valuable, or meaningful, or that we can't be attracted to them. Our relatives, our children, our friends and acquaintances—they are all valuable and important to us. But the word *love* should be reserved for one specific partner. In general conversation you can also 'love' your dog, ice cream, or your new shoes—that's why it's important to make a distinction."

LEARNING TO COPE WITH DISAPPOINTMENTS AND BETRAYALS

It's a good idea to try to figure out how we feel about the people around us. Is a friend from the office really a friend? Is a sexual relationship love, friendship, or something else although?

I asked the group, "What is the most personal and intimate relationship you can have with another person?"

Vicky jumped right in: "Well, true love is certainly the most intimate relationship. That's part of the reason it can only be shared with one other person."

"So what happens when the love for this person changes into more negative, destructive feelings?" I asked.

"We've all been there! When true love is frustrated or disappointed, hate takes over," Vicky answered.

"I think it's important to understand exactly what hate is. Let's try and think if we believe that in every love relationship a disappointment must lead to hatred.

"I want to describe to you a behavior I've observed in myself. I don't normally experience feelings of hatred, but once I was shocked to find that I had been used and betrayed in a relationship. I began to experience a feeling I'd never had before: hatred. In spite of that I still believe hatred to be an irrational feeling. But there it was, and I felt it for about ten days. I couldn't help myself. I could only observe how this strange and childish emotion had developed and taken root. Through that experience I came to realize that hatred is a feeling that develops when you discover that someone you loved has betrayed you. But how does one feel when one is betrayed?"

Julie felt that it was like an injury. She said she felt demoralized and discouraged when someone behaved so cruelly.

I was of the same opinion. "So we can say that hatred develops primarily when disappointment comes from being discouraged. A disappointment alone is unfortunate and leads to disillusionment, but it can only become hatred when we experience it as a painful injury. We need both elements—disappointment and discouragement—to develop hatred.

"Is there a way we can free ourselves of hatred? Hate doesn't do any good—it only ruins our health—so the question becomes: How can you overcome a disappointment or a discouragement?"

"Well, you have to be able to be angry," thought Charlie.

"What does 'being angry' mean? To throw everything away? Our emotions don't let themselves be manipulated that easily. The psyche is not a blackboard. You can't write on it and then erase your writing at will. There is only one way to dissolve feelings of hatred. You have to deal with the event and place it in context. We have to force ourselves to see reality as it really is. We have to give up our comfortable wishes of how we want it to be. Once we've managed to make ourselves face reality, then we've freed ourselves of disappointment. An injury is an expression of the other person's behavior. It needn't make a mark on how we feel about ourselves. It has nothing to do with our self-esteem and we shouldn't pay any attention to it."

"Does that mean that when my partner does something hurtful, I should just deal with it?" asked Vicky.

"When you say 'just deal with it,' what do you have in mind? Do you mean that you should just tolerate the behavior or do you mean that you should accept the situation for what it is and handle it accordingly?"

"No, I just mean that you should discuss the matter with your partner, and then handle the situation based on your discussion," Vicky answered.

"That's how I see it. That is how we get rid of the hate,

with which we would only end up hurting ourselves. That's what I meant when I said we should place the event in the context of reality. This is not a passive patience or tolerance; it's an active ordering of the situation. This means that with the person in question trust is no longer possible, and as a result neither love nor friendship are options.

"You might ask why even true friendship isn't possible. Well, what is a true friend? What prerequisites must a person fulfill in order to be a true friend of ours?"

Charles felt that he needed to be able to trust that person, and that the person could trust him.

Julie added, "It can't be a tit-for-tat situation—you shouldn't be in it for profit of any kind. When you want to be friends with someone because you hope to gain business or financial benefits, then that's not a friendship. The expression 'business friend' has always bothered me. You don't use your friends to make business deals, and you also don't abuse your relationship by using whatever business or social clout they might have. A friendship isn't about profiting from mentioning their name or by being seen with them. It always drives me crazy when I hear people saying things like 'My friend Senator X,' or 'My friend Professor Y.' You can't develop a friendship if you're only interested in the other person's social standing or business connections."

I continued, "That's a good reason why true friendships are few and far between, and why you can only ever have a handful of good friends. I think that in our society, where money, sex, and social prestige play such huge roles, most people never experience the happiness of a true friendship. Most people include their fellow students, their teammates, their acquaintances, and their drinking buddies in their circle of friends. You usually find out how wrong you are to consider them your friends as soon as you need their support. At this point it would be interesting to discuss what kind of feelings develop when a friendship goes bad. Imagine that a friend of yours, whom you trusted completely, betrays you. How do you feel about him now?"

"I hate him," Charles said forcefully.

Julie jumped in: "No, wait. This is not the kind of love relationship we were discussing earlier. When a friend of mine, or anyone who I consider a friend, hurts me and betrays me, then I'm just disgusted."

"Yes, Julie, that's exactly the word I would use to describe this experience. A demoralizing disappointment in love brings hatred. A demoralizing disappointment in friendship arouses disgust. It's pretty important, in any relationship, to decide whether it's love, friendship, or something else you're dealing with.

"There are other kinds of strong relationships that

aren't exactly love or friendship. We can feel a strong bond with someone because we share an ideal or an interest. Those that feel bound to another person by ideals or interests, and whose bond becomes exclusive of everyone else, are building a partnership or a community. I would consider political parties or religions to be such partnerships."

Charles added that the importance of these partnerships or communities was not to be underestimated, because he felt that they strongly influence how a certain person thinks or how he lives his life.

"It's a wonder, then, that a person from one such community can understand a person from another community," I observed.

Charles added, "That's exactly the reason why communities or partnerships that have different ways of thinking have a tendency to fight each other or even try to eradicate each other—"

"No," I interrupted, "that's not quite what I meant. Differences of thought, belief, or attitude do make it difficult to understand one another, but they don't necessarily make enemies of people. Catholics, Protestants, Jews and Muslims, Caucasians, people of color, teetotalers, and vegetarians could gain a great deal of personal growth and inspiration from each other if they only let themselves. Many who belong to a particular community feel that they are somehow better than others. Then they begin to designate themselves as an academic, or a member of the Rotary Club, or a VIP, or a philosopher, as a football fan, or as a member of a particular religion, or of a nation or of any other group.

"This kind of association can have serious consequences. The relationships between two groups can become nothing more than brutal intolerance."

Charles added, "I feel that terrorists, neo-Nazis, skinheads, and so forth are exactly that kind of intolerant and aggressive group. They've decided that they're really something special, and that they're better than anyone else. They think they're pretty cool when they demean Jewish identity or mistreat foreigners."

"You're exactly right," I answered. "When we talk about racism, xenophobia, and anti-Semitism, we shouldn't be content with identifying these behaviors; we should also get to the bottom of them.

"The cause for these behaviors is not simply hatred toward a particular victim. It's quite the opposite: The cause is the aggressiveness of the perpetrator. From his aggressive viewpoint the perpetrator looks for his victim. If he wants to cover up his acts with some sort of moral ideals, then he makes sure he provokes his victim, or claims that he's been provoked."

Charles agreed with me. "That's exactly how aggressive people behave—they provoke you until you have no choice but to fight. Until now, I've never quite seen the issue this clearly: taking an aggressive position against the repercussions of that same aggression. If you separate this issue in this way, you can control the aggression and prevent it from becoming a brutal or destructive action."

I was pleased with Charles's argument. "I think you're making a very important point. Anger, spite, jealousy, hate—these are all forms of our own aggression. You're either able to overcome these feelings and recapture a balance, or you commit aggressive acts and make your life difficult.

"When you haven't learned to distinguish the inner and outer circles, and you haven't managed to bring your self-image back to wholeness, harmony, and balance, then you need to at least try and vent your aggressions in a nondamaging way. However, you must be careful not to take these frustrations out on yourself by abusing alcohol or other drugs.

"There are harmless ways to ease anxieties and frustrations. You can clear up your aggressions through sports, good long walks, games, music, reading, or even by watching TV.

"It's important to create these vents in order to diminish the heavy toll that excesses of aggression take on us: poor health, criminal behavior, even war.

"Aggressive groups have a tendency to see themselves as a community of special people. They seek out weaker or somehow opposing outsiders as victims.

"It is not the victim who is at the root of this brutal intolerance. The real cause lies in the pressure for validation coming from within the community. It's this pressure for validation that leads to provocation and aggression. Words aren't the only way you can provoke someone. It's sometimes enough to be wearing flashy clothing to provoke someone who's looking for provocation."

Charles continued, "If all of these behaviors come from a need or a pressure for validation, then we need to know what the causes of this pressure are in order to understand the aggression that ultimately develops."

"That's exactly the question we need to clear up. The need or pressure for validation, like any excess, is grounded in its opposite. This pressure develops when a person or group suffers from a deficit of some kind. This deficit is rarely a material lack; rather it's the belief that we're somehow at a disadvantage or that we're not getting enough attention."

"That's right," Charles interjected. "A lot of people go through a lot of trouble to get attention, and then they complain that they aren't getting enough acknowledgment from others."

"Why do we need attention and acknowledgment? My answer is this: because we can't pay enough attention to ourselves. We need acknowledgment because we can't bring ourselves to approve of our own unfulfilling lives. A lot of people realize that they're egotistical, unfair, or insensitive, but they don't recognize that until they let go of these behaviors they'll never be free of a sense of unhappiness or worthlessness.

"The pressure for validation serves as a way to separate ourselves from others, to put ourselves in a higher class. Once you've distanced yourself, you can then treat others as worthless, demoralize them, or even hate them. Then they can be the scapegoat for your own sense of worthlessness.

"The feeling of worthlessness is unbearable, so we try anything in order to be free of it. In the aggressive groups and communities we were discussing, there's a great pressure to forget these feelings of worthlessness through acts of aggression. The great ideals that such groups claim to support are nothing more than a cosmetic illusion or even just a pretext. It's naive not to see through these claims and to let them excuse aggressive actions.

"Our goal here is not to compete in mental acrobatics. Rather, we need to see the circumstances clearly. We want to bring clarity into our relationships to others. It's pretty important to clear up our own relationships with others and to see them objectively. Is a relationship love or friendship? Is it friendship or a partnership/community because we follow the same ideal or have the same interests? When two people get together to fulfill their sexual needs, then it's neither love nor friendship—it's a 'special-interest partnership,' but certainly not what we've come to understand as love. It's a rude awakening when one partner finds that the relationship he or she thought was love is nothing more than a sexual convenience for the other partner. It's equally distressing when you believe you're friends with someone, while to them the relationship is nothing more than a special-interest partnership."

At this point Julie spoke up. "I still feel that many relationships have some connection to love. The value we bestow on another person—we've called it respectful love—can also come about in friendships or communities. Am I right?"

"Yes, you are. This kind of respectful love for others certainly exists, but we need to give it its own name. How can we name this kind of loving attitude, based in respect, that we can have toward an individual, a group, an institution, or even for all of nature?"

"Respect," offered Charles.

"Care," suggested Michael.

" 'No, it's definitely responsibility,' as my friend C. J. would say."

C. J. is a brilliant businessman who has brought his company to the top of its field. He feels a great deal of responsibility toward his business, his employees, his customers, and even toward the quality of his product and its environmental repercussions. It is exactly this sense of responsibility that has brought him so much success.

"It so happens that responsibility is the perfect name for respectful love in all of its manifestations. Any kind of respectful love brings responsibility into the picture."

THE RESPONSIBILITIES OF LOVE

Having determined that the respectful love we desired could be called responsibility, I guided the group into a discussion of the responsibilities of love.

"Responsibility is not a limited, intellectual answer to a single question, rather it is the real, emotional, and rational answer to all of our relationships.

"We often don't fully realize that we are responsible for two worlds: the inner world, which we denote by using the word *I*, and the outer world. Awareness of ourselves and our opinion of the outer world is part of the inner world. Our inner world is also the center of our spiritual guidance or direction.

"The other world is the material, outer world. We experience it with our senses, and we touch it with our hands or manipulate it with tools like hammers and robots, or even instruments such as electron microscopes and telescopes. Responsibility is part of both worlds. Our first responsibility is to ourselves. Our greatest responsibility is how we lead our lives. This responsibility involves how we live physically, and it influences our spiritual health.

"We have a secondary responsibility to those near us, our children, our friends. Responsibility to our children means treating them with the kind of respectful love we've discussed before. Responsibility to our friends means being sincere and reliable. Responsibility to those who are ill or the elderly means treating them with respect and understanding. When you take on a position of leadership, or if you have some kind of power, then you also take on additional responsibilities.

"C. J. always says that one of the hardest things in business is balancing the interests of the firm and the needs and desires of employees and clients. Responsibility to your employees is not just about fair pay, it's about creating an atmosphere of openness and building mutual trust.

"Not too many large corporations see it that way. Those who are out to make a fast buck, without too much foresight, have the erroneous idea that responsibility has negative consequences. This is why so many big businesses are more interested in maximizing profit rather than optimizing it. This attitude puts the workforce in an awkward position. Workers are constantly worried about downsizing, early retirement plans, layoffs, or the pressures of changing management. These are conditions under which the all-important mutual trust between employees and managers is easily disrupted.

"Those who are ambitious believe that a rise in profits will improve everyone's quality of life. Financial gain as a primary goal is emotionally miserly. Unfortunately, most individuals in upper management don't think this way.

"On the other hand, a responsible management will take care to successfully balance all four of the basic issues: financial gain for the firm, happiness and development of employees, customer satisfaction, and attention to environmental repercussions of the business.

"Social status within an institution, such as a high dignitary or politician may have, brings with it a set of responsibilities. When a king gets divorced or when a politician is caught lying, the image people have of him is broken—and so is trust.

"Naturally, we also have a responsibility to future generations in terms of the environment. Responsibility to nature demands use, but not abuse, of our resources. People in touch with nature have a harmonious relationship with the environment; they understand that the principle of give-and-take applies also in this realm. Balinese farmers give yearly offerings of flowers to the palm trees for their gift of the coconut. This is an example of showing a respectful love for nature."

"I find that, specifically toward nature, it's our duty to protect it and not allow it to be further destroyed," said Charles.

"Do you love nature?" I asked him.

"Yes. The older I get, the more important it becomes."

"If you really love nature, then it is your desire, and not a duty, to treat it lovingly and respectfully." Once I had said this, Charles realized that he had been confusing duty with responsibility.

In order to underline this point I continued, "You take responsibility because of a personal conviction. This is why true responsibility makes us happy. Duty, on the other hand, is literally a chore."

I told the group about my experiences in the military: "When I was a cadet, I was often given the most tiresome, almost ridiculous, chores, like spit-polishing a bicycle until it shone. Most of the time my superiors also added that it was 'my responsibility' to do these things well. To avoid getting in trouble I suppressed the answer I would gladly have given: 'It is not my responsibility; it is my duty.' Duty can be thrown at you when you're part of a dependent relationship. Responsibility, on the other hand, is something we take on voluntarily and because of our convictions.

"It is not a duty to care for our bodies through balanced nutrition and exercise—nobody can make us do it. We do it out of responsibility. We want to be healthy. Responsibility for ourselves applies not only to physical health, but also to the maintenance of a mental and spiritual balance. How do we achieve this balance?

"One of the most important questions we should ask ourselves is: What kind of thinking is the healthy, spiritual way of thinking?"

"You should try to think positive," offered Sam.

"That's what I think too," I answered. "But what do I mean by 'positive'?"

Charles answered, "To think positively is to be reasonably optimistic."

Michael disagreed. "Charles seems to think we have to run around wearing rose-colored glasses."

"If Sam had really meant that positive thinking meant optimism, I would not have agreed with him. Sam, you've studied Latin, right? What is the meaning of *positive*?"

"Positive comes from the Latin *ponere,* which means 'to place, lay, set.' "

"That's how I remembered it. So *positive* actually means 'settled.' The positive is simply how things really are. To think positively means to take reality for what it is and to handle things accordingly. A positive approach acknowledges reality but doesn't try to improve it through optimism. That would not be positive thinking—it would be an illusion. Spiritual and mental health are therefore based in a realistic way of thinking—about ourselves, about other people, and about society. The Roman emperor Marcus Aurelius was quite right when he said, 'Our life is what our thoughts make it.' "

CULTIVATING A HEALTHY SELF-IMAGE AND FINDING YOUR INNER BALANCE

It was Julie's turn to speak. "I am convinced that spiritual well-being is essential to physical health, to the maintenance of physical processes, and even to healing and recovery."

"That makes a lot of sense," agreed Michael. "Research has shown that roughly one-third of illnesses are brought on by psychosomatic factors. But as a physician, how do I help my patients achieve this inner balance? Or if we want to avoid that mystifying term *inner,* how do I help them achieve a harmonious relationship with themselves?"

Michael is a particularly sensitive physician. I thought I should ask him the following: "Do you heal your patients, or do you arm them with the necessary weapons to heal their own bodies?"

"Naturally the body heals itself. I'm at least that realistic."

"So how does it work with the inner balance we're discussing? Is there a shot or a pill for it?" I continued.

"All right, I get it. The patient must find her own balance. You're alluding to the example of the bicycle!" Michael beamed like a prize student.

He was referring to the bicycle example in my book *The Four Color Man*. I told the group, "I'll repeat the story for you here, since you're probably not familiar with it.

"Since pictures speak a thousand words, let me use a visual example of inner balance. Can you remember when you learned to ride a bike?

"First you need a bicycle. We'll compare this vehicle to our bodies and hereditary factors. There are light racing bikes and massive old clunkers; there are elegant shiny new bikes or rusty old scraps. Sometimes you can even get a bike that was damaged at the factory, just as you might have negative or destructive hereditary factors. The rules of the road are like the rules of social conduct and the society you live in. There are smooth and bumpy roads, some are always ready to surprise you with potholes, some climb steeply upwards, and some have such an incline that we end up riding the brakes or crashing. The most important thing is you, the bike rider. You've been taught to push on the pedals to make the bicycle move. We'll compare this to our daily activities. If you aren't pedaling, pushing yourself, being active, then you're going to fall on your face. If you try to zoom off with an explosive start, you risk losing balance and falling over.

"You've also been taught how to turn right and left, and how to go straight. Turning is like our intention to steer toward a specific goal.

"A patient teacher will show you all of these things. You know, however, that even the best bike (heredity), the most convenient road rules (social rules), the strongest push (activity), and the most skillful steering (goal orientation), won't get you from here to there if you can't fulfill the one requirement that can't be taught. Your teacher can run next to you or hold you in balance on the seat, but this is the only help he or she can offer. Eventually you'll have to reach the point where you can do it alone. Suddenly you find that you're in balance, and that you can keep that balance. You take great pains to maintain that balance, or to find it quickly should you lose it."

Michael spoke up. "The example of the bicycle is very nice, but still most people are not able to reach psychological balance through spiritual growth. I'm convinced of the importance of spiritual health, but how do I achieve it? What do I need to do in order to retain inner balance?"

There was a pause in the conversation, so I posed the following question: "Do you have any idea why so many people who aren't lacking for material goods suffer and damage themselves both physically and spiritually?

"People who feel dependent, or somehow emotionally bound, remain fearful. They are spiritually and emotionally blocked. This kind of life doesn't bring any happiness. It's a condition of toil and suffering. What causes it?"

Julie came up with a possible answer. "They suffer as adults because they grew up in negative circumstances. I'm thinking of conflicts at home such as a divorce. Our conspicuous consumerism, violence on television, sensationalist news—all of these outside influences can disturb people and make them unhappy."

"Do they have to?" I asked. "I think that's too easy an explanation. It also doesn't quite answer the question. I think the cause of our unhappiness lies within ourselves. The French philosopher Montaigne said, 'A man doesn't suffer because of outside pressures—he suffers because of how he handles them.'

"Let's take two men, for example. Both men's girlfriends leave them for some new stud. The first man thinks to himself, Well, if she didn't love me, she isn't worth it, and the other one turns into a jealous stalker. As you can see, it all depends on how you handle an event."

As I was speaking, an experience came to me that I thought I ought to share. It had really changed my life.

"Many years ago I was sitting by the lake and feeding the gulls. When a piece of bread fell in the water, all the gulls fell upon the bread at once. Finally one of the gulls yanked the bread out of the mouth of another gull. What would a person do when faced with this kind of rudeness? We would yell, or start a fight, or at the very least feel deeply offended. A gull doesn't behave so stupidly. The gull doesn't go off into a corner feeling sorry for itself—it moves on and prepares to catch the next piece of food.

"Suddenly it became clear to me that this situation happens over and over again in our own minds. The anger, the pain, the disappointment, I create these feelings by myself and, more importantly, *for* myself. I not only make myself angry, I disappoint myself as well."

"Is that the mistake I'm making when I get angry or disappointed?" asked Julie, wanting to make sure she'd understood my point.

"I'm convinced of it," I agreed, and continued, "I make myself angry. I only *believe* that I'm angry about something or because of someone. I should say I make myself angry and use someone else as an excuse."

Julie wanted to make sure she was following my argument. "So I'm wrong to be angry that someone else has made a mess or screwed up, even when I've warned him? But isn't it human to get mad?"

"Human, yes, but also stupid. When someone makes a mess of a task you've set them to, and you get mad, you're actually getting mad because you've expressed yourself unclearly, or because you've asked an inexperienced person to do something. You're actually getting mad with yourself. Try and see, next time you get mad, if that isn't the case."

"Naturally the anger comes from me. I end up hurting myself, I realize that much. But should I never get mad?" Julie continued.

"No, not even an animal is stupid enough to get angry," I insisted. "Anger keeps us from exercising good judgment and handling situations appropriately. Anger closes the doors to reality. Observing the wakeful attention of animals, you realize that they live in undeniable reality and they are able to react quickly and honestly to any event.

"We humans often don't live in the real world at all. We live in the world that we call 'I.' This 'I' world is the warehouse of imagination. I imagine I look good, or that I am not at all attractive. I feel terrific and highly regarded, or I feel insecure and worthless. These kinds of evaluations run through our minds daily. We're constantly trying to measure how others perceive us.

"These are all images that we construct in our own minds. We seem to want these images to convince us, so we run them over and over in our heads. Unfortunately, they're almost always wrong. You might be convinced that you have an ugly nose, but someone out there is bound to find it attractive."

"I've experienced that directly," said Julie. "I always thought my nose was small and pug, but when I was in school many of my fellow students used to tell me how attractive they thought it was."

I repeated my argument: "All of these images separate us from reality. They wall us into that imaginary 'I' world. We make our ego the center of the world instead of reality. When we've gone too far we can be described with a pretty ugly word: *egocentric*. We're constantly dancing around our precious 'I.' Sometimes we're afraid that nobody loves us, so we either block ourselves from making contact at all or we try to make others love us by feeling sorry for us. Sometimes this behavior even makes us look ridiculous."

"But when someone else disappoints us, then it can't always be our fault, can it?" Julie asked. "Disappointment must work differently."

"Think carefully about what you're saying. When you're disappointed it means that you had some kind of expectation that wasn't fulfilled. The disappointment breaks the expectation and shows you the reality. Disappointment discourages you from building unrealistic expectations. Even though it's tough at first, we should be happy not to be chasing false expectations.

"Would you rather be deluded and following dreams and expectations, or be in touch with reality and experience it how it really is? I think that dealing with reality makes life easier," I concluded and looked at the completely bewildered faces around me. I pressed on. "I have learned to be happy that I have been disappointed, freed from false expectations."

Julie smiled to herself and eventually murmured, "That's ridiculous. We all live in a crazy world of pure expectation. You're right, *egocentric* is a negative word. With all of the moralizing value judgments we make, we make our own lives hell."

Michael was triumphant. "You see, the Bible is right. Once we started judging wrong and right—since Adam and Eve bit from the fruit of the tree of knowledge—we've been banished from Paradise. We have to stop judging everything and making ourselves angry about it."

Julie had a concern about this. "That's all well and good, but what about those who have a family to feed and can't just quit their jobs? Or what can you do if you're constantly being unfairly blamed by your partner but can't leave because of the children? Shouldn't you make a judgment? Shouldn't you get mad?"

Julie's question reminded me of a drawing I had used in my book *The Four Color Man*. This drawing helps me to find balance when something has disturbed me. I took a pen and drew a circle the size of a coin on one of the paper napkins on our table.

"Let's imagine that we are this circle. The circle is the 'I' we've been talking about. We have to be careful for our entire lives that the circle remains round and harmonious."

Then I drew a second, dented and battered, circle around the first, and continued. "The dented circle is the world around us that we experience every day. The outer world is never perfectly round—there's always a dent here or there. These are the problems and concerns of daily life that often make us angry. The outer circle also has some smooth curves—these are our successes.

"I take great care to keep the inner 'I' circle separated from the outer.

"Unfortunately, children, and immature adults, are unable to make this division. Whether something goes well or goes wrong in the outer circle, their inner circle is affected. They damage their self-image, they feel wounded, hurt, angry, or insecure.

"A mature person has learned that failures, but also successes, must not bend the inner circle. It must remain smooth and round at all costs. As soon as we realize that we're disappointed or angry or injured, we have to go back to the inner circle and make sure it stays round and harmonious.

"Our normal self-image, our confidence, our happiness, and especially our self-esteem should never be influenced by the outer circle."

Julie volunteered an example. "Recently I got really mad about something. A young patient of mine, while lying on an X-ray table, grabbed my breast as I leaned over him."

I asked her to think if the young man's action had somehow damaged her self-esteem.

"Naturally it didn't. That kind of crap has nothing to do with my self-esteem," she answered emphatically.

"Exactly. The outer event had nothing to do with your self-image."

Michael broke in. "But if someone calls me a jerk, then that comment was made to be hurtful, to wound me."

"That's true. That's how it was meant. The question is whether you should let it bother you. If your inner and outer worlds are sufficiently separated, then that kind of offense shouldn't affect you. I don't think I'm a jerk, even if I make a mistake. Even if I did think so, I shouldn't feel offended. It would be illogical, unrealistic, just plain wrong, to let offensive remarks into my inner circle, into my self-image. It also follows that these things shouldn't disappoint us or upset us. Do you remember my story about the gulls?"

Julie and Michael answered yes in unison. Michael continued, "The story of the gulls made me realize that whatever disappointments, anger, or hurt we experience we produce ourselves. We always see that the other person has hurt us, or disappointed us. You're right. We think that the feelings developed in the outer circle belong in the inner circle, that they somehow take place in the 'I.' Your example has really made a lot of personal sense."

I asked, "Why do the gulls have no problem with their inner circles? Do you know?" The answer was in the air—Michael had already all but given it—it only took my question to push him a little farther to it.

"Oh, I see! The gulls don't have an inner circle in which to be angry. They don't have an 'I' that can feel hurt or disappointed. Does that mean that our 'I' is the root of all the problems?"

I was pleased with his question. "Yes, you could put it that way. I just want to say it a little more clearly: The gulls' 'I' is not a circle, but a tiny dot in the center of a circle. It's called the subject. Every life-form is a subject. Gulls, and most other animals, react directly from this point to the outer world. They don't have the complication of the inner circle. That way they live completely spontaneously and undeniably in reality.

"People, unlike animals, are blocked from the outer world by the inner circle. This inner circle interferes with the middle point (the subject) and the outer circle.

"The images we create of ourselves are almost always

an illusion. Some fool themselves into a feeling of over-importance. Others often feel insecure and hesitant. All of these images create an inner circle that isn't round at all, but rather completely twisted and obscured by our own misconceived notions of ourselves and how the rest of the world perceives us. These 'I' images are nothing more than caricatures. It's like seeing yourself in a distorted mirror. When we repeat these images to ourselves on a daily basis, we begin to believe they're true. This makes it very difficult to get away from them. Unfortunately, when there's no inner harmony, we cannot develop a harmonious relationship with the outside."

"The inner circle is an unbelievable thing," said Julie. "The 'I' circle contains all of the elements of human tragedy: the frustrations and aggressions, the illusions and depressions. All of that comes from inside our heads. You should clear this up for yourself once and for all. To be angry, hurt, disappointed, unhappy, the need to feel worthy—all of this presumption creates frustration. In turn, every frustration brings either sadness or aggression or illusionary hopes."

"Can you take that one step farther?" I asked. "Without such bent 'I' circles, there wouldn't be any crime, any hate, and ideological intolerance. There wouldn't be any politically or religiously motivated violence and brutality.

"We have to learn to feel the laws of harmony within

us. They're our inner compass. They tell us the way to make the right decisions.

"When we've developed our inner circle—hence our self-esteem and confidence—to a harmonious level, then the relationships to the outer circle, to reality, will naturally follow this lead."

Julie thought about it for a moment with her eyes focused on some distant point. Then she began, "Now I understand what we mean when we talk about inner freedom. It means to be free of the illusions I've created about myself. I must discover all of these self-imposed prejudices that close me in. I have to find and get rid of all of these false images that twist and dent my inner circle. I want to be free of those pressures and finally live as naturally and spontaneously as I have always felt I should. I want to be internally free. I'm tired of making myself dependent on inconsequential things."

"What you've just shown us is already a spontaneous and free understanding. But it takes daily practice to truly find inner freedom. We need to always be aware if we're deceiving ourselves or making opportunistic concessions. Most importantly, we need to have the courage to follow our true wishes. Only action makes us free. Confidence can only grow from action and its successes.

"Do you know why people continue making themselves unhappy and captive? Why do so many of us need an idol or a talisman or an ideology to hold on to? Why do we give ourselves over to people—politicians, bosses, gurus—who misuse our belief and make us into their little acolytes? Why do so many of us willingly give ourselves over to spiritual dependence?

"By making yourself dependent, you're not only taking away your own freedom, you're also damaging your faith in yourself. By making yourself dependent, you're corrupting yourself and you also manipulate the people whom you make dependent on you."

Charles broke in. "I understand that inner freedom is important for self-confidence and self-esteem. I also understand that I can only be happy when my inner circle is in harmony. But if everything is so harmonious, won't I get bored?"

"That's a good question. Unfortunately, many people feel that harmony must be one long, boring lifetime of peaceful rest and inactivity. Harmony is actually the *act* of making sure that all of the elements of one's busy life can flow smoothly together: everything from work to romance to family to whatever you do to relax."

Julie nodded thoughtfully, then addressed me. "When everything flows smoothly and harmoniously and life becomes so balanced, won't it lose some of its richness and vitality? I mean if nothing is happening—if there's no crisis brewing or no promise of something great about to happen—then there's nothing left to get excited about."

"In a sense you're right—it wouldn't be quite so exciting. But you're wrong to believe that life would lose its richness. Quite the opposite: It would be richer. All of the empty actions that waste our time and our mental and physical energy—like looking for a romance with a partner who is ultimately the wrong match—become unnecessary and fall away. Once we can recognize the useless, time-wasting endeavors and jettison them, we can experience the good things more intensely and will be able to focus on life's rich rewards. Life isn't enriched by what we own or what's going on. It's enriched by what we experience with sensitivity, happiness and, if we're lucky, true love."

ABOUT THE AUTHOR

Dr. Max Lüscher studies philosophy, psychology, and psychiatry in Basel. His Color Diagnostic Theory has found worldwide recognition, and has been translated into twenty-seven languages. Max Lüscher has taught his Color Diagnostic Theory in numerous universities in Western and Eastern Europe, as well as at Yale University and in Australia. He works as a psychotherapist and as a consultant to various top international businesses. Much of his work is in education of physicians and businessmen. For decades his books have been best-sellers around the world. Other works by Dr. Lüscher include *The Lüscher Color Test*, *Signals of Personality*, *The Four Color Man*, *Team Harmony*, *Lüscher Diagnostic*, and *The Lüscher Cube*.